The New Webster's
COMPUTER
HANDBOOK

By Jenny Tesar, M.S.

LEXICON PUBLICATIONS, INC.

Editor: Jeffrey H. Hacker

Design and Illustration: Walter A. Schwarz

ISBN: 0-7172-4659-0

CONTENTS

WHO USES COMPUTERS — AND WHY?

Chapter One

INTRODUCTION TO COMPUTERS

It wasn't too many years ago that computers seemed far removed from ordinary, everyday life. Today, however, computers are everywhere. Millions of small personal computers (pc's) are installed in homes, offices, factories, churches, government agencies, auto repair shops, cruise ships, schools, stores, and restaurants. Five-year-old kids use pc's. Retired people use them. Artists, postal clerks, physicians, soldiers, florists, engineers, and tennis coaches use them.

You've probably heard the term "computer literate." A person who is computer literate understands computers, their functions, and how to use them. This doesn't mean the person knows how to build computers or is able to create the programs used by computers. It simply means that the person:

- Recognizes the roles that computers play in today's world — and in his or her own life
- Knows how to get a computer to do the tasks he or she wants it to do.

In other words, being computer literate is very much like being telephone literate!

When you are computer literate, you have definite advantages. You can accomplish tasks quicker and more accurately. You have a better shot at being hired for good, well-paying jobs — and being promoted to higher positions. You are more likely to get and retain customers and clients.

WHO USES COMPUTERS — AND WHY?

Computers have revolutionized the way that people work. Interior designers now use computers to estimate the costs of remodeling jobs. Farmers use them to milk cows. Astronomers use them to study distant stars. Truckers use them to stay in touch with company headquarters. Choreographers use them to create new dances. Civil engineers use them to study how bridges will act in windstorms and earthquakes. Mapmakers use them to update maps. Teachers use them to help children learn arithmetic.

Computers also have revolutionized the way that companies operate. Telephone companies use computers to find the best routing for long-distance calls. Travel agencies use computers to peruse airline schedules and fares, check hotel offerings, and reserve rental cars. Music companies use computerized recording and reproduction technologies to make tapes and CD-ROMs of your favorite singers. Hospitals use CAT scans (Computerized Axial Tomography) to give physicians detailed looks inside a patient's body. Flight schools use computers during flight training, to let student pilots experience simulated crashes, mechanical failures, and other emergency situations.

As you go about your everyday chores, you frequently interact with computers. At the supermarket, a clerk uses a computerized scanner to total your purchases and print out a sales slip. At the bank, a teller uses a computer to process your transactions. At the library, you use a computer to learn if the latest mystery by your favorite author is available. At a fast-food restaurant, you use a computer to place your order.

And even if you think you don't own a computer, you probably do. You may not have a computer sitting on your desk, or a lightweight computer tucked into a briefcase, but you probably have several embedded computers. These are computers installed in other machines to make the machines work more efficiently.

Perhaps you have a thermostat that you can preset to maintain a daytime temperature of 68 degrees and a nighttime temperature of 60 degrees. Once you enter these instructions into the thermostat, a tiny computer inside the thermostat automatically causes your heating system to turn on and off so that the desired temperatures are maintained.

If you've recently bought a sewing machine, chances are it's computerized. Simply press a button and you can to make button-holes, embroider flowers, or stitch a row of bumblebees. Telephones, VCRs, food processors, microwave ovens, watches, and automobiles are among the thousands of other products that have embedded computers.

Basic Functions

Computers increase productivity — for both individuals and organizations — because:

- They are fast
- They are accurate
- They can process huge amounts of information
- They eliminate boring work
- They are inexpensive.

Even though computers are amazingly versatile, the wide variety of tasks they perform can be grouped into five basic functions:

Manipulate numbers Computers can rapidly solve all sorts of numerical problems. Even computers small enough to be easily carried in a shoulder bag can perform tens of thousands of calculations every second without error.

One familiar arithmetic problem that is better handled by computers than by hand is the preparation of expense reports and other information needed for filing tax documents. This can be a very time-consuming chore when done by hand. You have to enter hundreds of figures on paper spreadsheets, then use a calculator or pencil and paper to obtain your totals. Whoops! You forgot to include an expense for last January. After you plug in this expense, you must erase and retotal a long column of figures. On an electronic spreadsheet, such totals are handled automatically by the computer. Instead of spending many minutes to correct an error, the error is corrected in less than a second.

Organize and analyze information Computers can keep track of any kind of information, organize it in meaningful ways, and display it in various ways to help you perform analyses.

Imagine that you're the manager of a local softball league. You can use a pc to keep track of schedules, players, equipment, attendance figures, expenses, and income. You can graph changes in attendance, chart player stats, compare profit-and-loss statements for the past ten years, and forecast the affect on league finances of an increase in electric rates or plans to sell advertising on season schedules.

Store and retrieve information   Computers can store phenomenal amounts of information, or data, in a very small space. Once you've stored the data, you can use the computer to quickly find, or retrieve, it.

Let's say you have 943 customers. How do you keep track of their names, addresses, purchases, dates of purchases, and so forth? Do you have a manila file for each customer, and several file cabinets in which to store the files? How long would it take you to use this system to prepare a list of all your customers in Kansas? To rank them according to the value of their purchases? It would probably take you — or someone whose salary you're paying — quite a while.

Using a pc is much faster. Once you've entered the names of the customers into a computer database, you can store all the records on a few small disks. You can quickly add, change, remove, and analyze the information. If you want to know which customers are based in Kansas, just tell the computer to read the customer list and pull out the names of everyone in Kansas. In seconds, the list is displayed on the screen. Press a key on the computer keyboard, and you get a printout on paper of the list. Now ask the computer to rank these customers according to the dollar amount of purchases they made during the past year. In a flash, the new list appears on the screen. It, too, can be immediately printed.

Create and edit documents and pictures   Computers can be used to create letters, reports, books, airplane designs, room layouts — indeed, any kind of written or drawn material. As you create a document or picture, you can add to it, erase parts, or rearrange parts. When it's exactly the way you want it, you can save the final version in the computer for later use or you can print it on paper or send it via telephone to another computer.

WHAT CAN YOU DO WITH A HOME COMPUTER?

Access the computer in your office.
Build your vocabulary.
Create a customized vegetable garden.
Design greeting cards.
Evaluate stock options.
File your income tax return.
Get the latest weather reports.
Hear music.
Improve your typing skills.
Job hunt.
Keep track of how many calories you eat.
Learn a foreign language.
Maintain a list of household possessions.
Navigate a submarine in a simulated battle.
Organize your collection of baseball cards.
Pay bills.
Quickly update Christmas card lists.
Reserve an airline seat.
Send a fax.
Transfer money from one bank account to another.
Use computerized shopping services.
View a simulated rainforest.
Write letters.
X-amine mortgage options.
Yak with people in distant places.
Zoom through space in an arcade game.

No crossing out words and adding new ones, making your letter look messy. No misspellings that require you to carefully retype an entire page. And for artists, there's another benefit. If you want to show how a house looks from four different angles, you can produce four drawings by hand. Or you can use a computer to create one three-dimensional drawing, then instruct the computer to rotate the drawing to show the house from every possible angle!

Send and receive information Computers can be connected to one another via telephone lines or special cables. This enables a computer user to "talk" to other computer users, play games with them, and leave messages — called electronic mail — for them. It also enables computer users to connect to information services, which are broad-based collections of databases. For a fee, these services offer information ranging from the latest sports scores and stock quotes to first-aid remedies and synopses of recent scientific research. Yes, you could gather all this information from a combination of newspapers, books, tv reports, and technical journals, but it would take much, much longer.

LEARNING TO USE A COMPUTER

If you are just beginning to learn about computers, you are on the doorstep of an exciting — and FUN! — experience. Approach this experience with the same enthusiasm and expectations of success as you approached your first driving lessons, when you couldn't wait to get your driver's license!

You'll soon discover that learning how to use a computer is not difficult. Many of today's computers are carefully designed to be easy to use. It's not much more time consuming to learn how to write a letter on a computer than it is to learn how to use a typewriter. It's not much more difficult to learn how to keep your company's accounts receivable on a computer than it is to learn how to do this on paper.

Perhaps you already know how to do these tasks the "old-fashioned" way. Why take the time — and spend the money — to computerize? For the reasons already mentioned: you'll get the work done faster, more accurately, and at less cost. You'll also have options you didn't have before. Instead of an ordinary typewritten memo to employees or customers, you can use the computer to turn the memo into a classy, illustrated newsletter. Instead of driving prospective home buyers around to dozens of different houses, you can let them use a computer to see interior and exterior pictures of the houses, thereby eliminating time-consuming trips.

When you sit before a typewriter for the first time, you do not type 60 words per minute. When you pick up a paintbrush for the first time, you do not create a masterpiece. When you use water-skis or golf clubs or a tennis racket for the first time, you do not challenge the pros.

Similarly, it takes practice and patience to learn how to use computers. Start with a game or with simple, familiar tasks that you normally would complete manually, such as writing a letter or organizing a list of bank accounts. Learn how to turn the computer on and off, adjust the display screen, and use the keyboard and mouse.

Read the manuals that come with the computer. They usually present examples of introductory activities. Don't be afraid to experiment. And don't worry about making mistakes. Pressing the wrong key on the computer keyboard or the wrong button on a mouse won't hurt the computer!

Sources of Help

This book provides the basics you need to buy and begin using computers in your home and office. The manuals that come with computer equipment also contain valuable information on how to get the most out of your purchases.

There are many additional sources of help, some for beginners, others for people who have mastered the basics and wish to expand their knowledge and capabilities. Because of the rapid advances in computer technology, most people who use computers find it beneficial to continually educate themselves about computers and how to use them.

Classes Adult education programs in local schools frequently offer computer courses. Most common are introductory courses and courses that focus on specific applications, such as electronic spreadsheets and word processing. Computer stores in your community may hold classes, too. If you belong to a professional organization, it may offer workshops and continuing education courses on computer topics of particular interest to your industry.

Books New books on computers and computer applications are constantly being published; most bookstores and libraries devote clearly marked areas to these books. Because the computer industry changes so rapidly, books — like magazines — can quickly become outdated. It's often wise to check a book's copyright date and review its table of contents before buying it. Some books provide a general overview of computers and how to use them. Other books focus on leading you step by step through a computer application. Still others are filled with tips and tricks that help experienced users expand the capabilities of their system.

Magazines A wide variety of computer magazines are available through bookstores and other retail outlets, as well as in your local library and by subscription. Their information tends to be more up-to-date than the information in books. Some magazines are designed for beginning users, others are for experienced users, and still others are for people with technical knowledge. There are magazines that specialize in subjects such as computer networks, computer graphics, and computer games, as well as magazines that specialize in the use of computers in specific industries, such as education, medicine, and publishing.

Video tapes Instructional videos guide viewers step-by-step through the use of a computer or program. They may be particularly helpful if you want to provide a group of employees with a general introduction to computers or to a specific software program you are installing. Several companies offer videos on the most popular business software, such as *Lotus 1-2-3*, *Windows*, and *WordPerfect*.

User groups Many communities have computer user groups that you can join. A user group is a club that meets regularly to share ideas and information, hear presentations by experts, help one another solve problems, and so on. It's a great place for beginners to learn from experienced users. Some user groups are large enough to have subgroups organized around a particular product, such as Macintosh computers, or a particular application, such as computer networks.

Manufacturers Some manufacturers of computer products publish newsletters to keep their customers informed of new versions of the products, and to provide tips on how to use products more efficiently.

Consultants If you plan to automate your business, you may wish to hire a consultant to guide the buying process, oversee the installation, and teach you and your employees how to use the system.

HOW COMPUTERS WORK

A computer is a tool. Like a typewriter, tire jack, hammer, food blender, or any other tool, it's designed to do work. We've already looked at the kinds of work a computer does: calculating, organizing, communicating, analyzing, and so on.

The computer does all this work electronically. Every second, millions, even billions, of electric signals zip in and out of the computer's "brain" — its central processing unit.

The Central Processing Unit (CPU)

The computer's central processing unit, or CPU, contains thousands of electric circuits. Yet in a personal computer (pc), the entire CPU is built on a wafer of silicon about the size of your fingernail. Such a wafer is called a chip.

Chips are the building blocks of computers. There are many kinds of chips in a computer, each containing many electric circuits. The chip used for the CPU of a personal computer is called a microprocessor ("small processor").

The main functions of the CPU are to process information and act as the computer's traffic cop. It has two main parts:

Arithmetic and logic unit (A/LU) This is where all arithmetic and logical operations take place. Arithmetic operations involve adding, subtracting, multiplying, and dividing. Logical operations define the logical relationships between two quantitites or conditions. For example, the A/LU may compare two numbers to determine which is bigger. Or it may compare a value against an average to determine if the value is average, above average, or below average. All operations in the A/LU take place with lightning speed.

BUILDING BLOCKS OF MICROCOMPUTER SYSTEMS

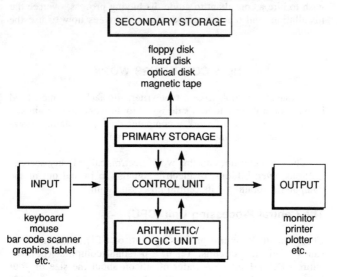

Control unit This is the traffic cop. It controls and coordinates all operations of the computer. It decides what the A/LU should do. It also transfers information to and from devices such as the printer and keyboard. Like the A/LU, it works phenomenally rapidly.

As you can see, computer processing involves three steps:

Input The CPU is given instructions about what to do
Processing The CPU does the work
Output The CPU sends out the results of its work.

Suppose you're writing a letter. You type the word *Hello* on the keyboard. Your action is an instruction to the CPU (input). It tells the CPU to write the word *Hello* and display it on the monitor screen so you can see it. The CPU interprets and follows your instructions (processing). You see the results of its work when Hello appears on the screen (output).

Computer Memory

Like humans, computers have memories. Their memories are used to store instructions and information.

Primary storage   This is where the computer holds instructions and information that it is currently using. This area is also known as *computer memory* or *temporary storage*. If you are writing a letter using a word processing program, the program and the letter are held here. Or, let's say you tell the computer to add 5 plus 7. The computer has to get these numbers from specified locations in memory. After the A/LU adds the numbers, the result is stored in another location in memory.

Secondary storage   Perhaps you want to store the letter and work on it again tomorrow. You cannot store it in primary storage because that memory is temporary. The computer "forgets" everything in primary storage when you turn it off. The letter has to be stored in so-called secondary storage. This is separate from the CPU. Information stored here will never be forgotten.

Computer Hardware

When people say they have a computer, they actually mean they have a computer system. They do not only have a computer with its CPU and memory chips. They also have various pieces of equipment that connect to the computer. These devices are called peripherals. There are three main types of peripherals:

Input devices   Used to enter information and instructions into the computer; examples include keyboards, mice, joysticks, and graphics tablets.

Output devices   Used to receive information from the computer; examples include monitors, printers, and speech synthesizers.

Storage devices   Used to store computer output so that it can be retrieved and used again at some future time; examples include disk drives, tape units, and CD-ROM.

In a sense, storage peripherals are combination input/output devices: they store computer output so that a person can input, or

A TYPICAL COMPUTER SYSTEM

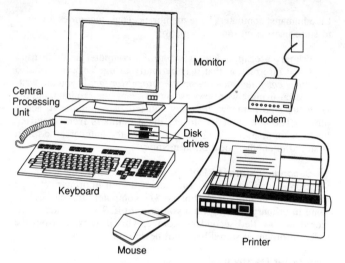

load, it into the computer again. Another input/output peripheral is the modem, a device that enables a computer to send and receive data through ordinary telephone lines.

Together, computers and peripherals are called hardware.

Connecting Hardware

Electrical paths link the components of a computer system so that they can communicate with one another. Some electrical paths, or conductors, are unidirectional; they can carry signals in one direction only. Other electrical conductors are bidirectional; they can carry signals in either direction.

Conductors that connect components within the computer itself are called buses. There are three main kinds of buses:

- Address buses enable the CPU to contact, or address, locations in memory and connections to peripherals.

- Control buses carry signals, such as signals that tell peripherals to get ready to send or receive data.
- Data buses carry information.

Circuits that connect the computer with peripherals are called interfaces. There are two main kinds of interfaces:

- Serial interfaces transmit data serially, one bit at a time.
- Parallel interfaces transmit a group of bits of data in parallel — that is, simultaneously.

Computer Software

By itself, computer hardware cannot perform work. It needs to be told what to do. A list of instructions that tells a computer how to perform a specific task is called a computer program, or software.

You're likely to use four types of software:

Operating systems   An operating system is a collection of programs that enables all the hardware in a computer system to work together. It also controls the running of other programs. It's like a traffic cop, coordinating input, output, and other processes. The operating system is either built into the computer or loaded into the computer's memory from a disk when you turn on the computer.

Utility programs   An operating system includes various utility programs; other utility programs can be purchased separately. These programs perform housekeeping and maintenance tasks, such as preparing a blank disk for use with your computer or recovering data that you accidentally erased.

Windowing environments   These are extensions of a computer's operating system. They enable a user to interact with the computer by selecting pictures or commands from the display screen instead of typing in commands. Pull-down menus, so named because they are "pulled down" from a bar at the top of the screen, present options from which you choose what you want.

Windowing environments make the computer "friendlier" and easier to use. They also give a person the ability to run two or

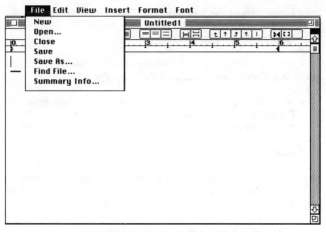

A TYPICAL PULL-DOWN MENU

more application programs simultaneously — a process called multitasking. Each application is shown in its own box, or window, on the screen.

Application programs These programs perform specific tasks that you want to accomplish, such as writing a letter, calculating taxes, creating an illustrated report, and having fun! They include word processing programs, database programs, spreadsheet programs, inventory-control programs, drawing programs, personal finance programs, educational programs, computer games, and many other kinds of programs.

The Binary System

To communicate with a computer, we have to speak its language. But a computer is like a light switch: it is made up of miniature electronic devices that can distinguish only two states: *on* and *off*. How is it possible to instruct the computers's circuits to do all sorts of complex tasks using only two words?

Computers use the binary system for all calculations and processing. The binary system is a numbering system that has only two digits: 0 and 1. (In comparison, the decimal system has ten digits: 0 through 9.) In the binary system, as shown in the chart, all numbers are expressed as combinations of 0 and 1.

All input (information entered into a computer) is translated by the computer into its working language of 0's and 1's, with each 0 representing *off* and each 1 representing *on*. The two numerals, 0 and 1, are called bits, which is a short form of binary digit. A group of eight bits is called a byte. A byte is the fundamental unit used by all computers.

Using a special code, it is possible to represent every letter, number, and other symbol (punctuation marks, dollar signs, parentheses, etc.) in our language by 8-bit numbers, or bytes. Indeed, there are enough 8-bit numbers left over to use some for commands, such as "leave a space here."

BINARY EQUIVALENTS OF DECIMAL NUMBERS 1 THROUGH 21

DECIMAL	BINARY	DECIMAL	BINARY	DECIMAL	BINARY
1	1	8	1000	15	1111
2	10	9	1001	16	10000
3	11	10	1010	17	10001
4	100	11	1011	18	10010
5	101	12	1100	19	10011
6	110	13	1101	20	10100
7	111	14	1110	21	10101

ASCII Code

In 1968, a group of manufacturers agreed to adopt a standard code, with a specific binary number representing a specific character or command. This agreement meant that data produced on one computer could be used on other kinds of computers, and could also be understood by printers, monitors, and other peripherals. The code is the American Standard Code for Information Interchange, or ASCII (pronounced *ass-key*).

Every letter, number, and other character that a computer can produce is represented by an agreed-upon ASCII code. There are 128 basic ASCII codes, from 000 to 127. This is called conventional ASCII. When you press a key on the keyboard, the three-digit code is sent to the central processing unit (CPU). For example, when you type a capital M, ASCII code 077 is sent.

There also is an extended set of codes, from 128 to 255. These codes are used to represent special characters, such as Greek symbols and accented letters found in foreign languages.

Almost all computer and software manufacturers around the world use the same definitions for ASCII codes 000 to 127, but they may use different definitions for codes 128 to 255. For example, the British pound symbol is code 156 in one standard but code 163 in another.

Some ASCII numbers are control codes. For example:

009   tab (signals the display screen to move the cursor to the next tab stop; can result from pressing the TAB key on the keyboard).

010   line feed (signals the printer to move the paper to the next line).

013   carriage return (signals the printer or the display screen to move the print head or cursor to the left-hand margin; can result from pressing the ENTER key on the keyboard).

028–031   cursor movements (signal the display screen to move the cursor: 028 = right, 029 = left, 030 = up, and 031 = down).

The importance of ASCII   ASCII can have important implications for your work. Let's say you're writing a report using a word processing program. When you type an M on the keyboard, ASCII enables the computer to quickly translate the M into electronic code that it stores in memory. Now let's say that you want to send the report via telephone to another pc. This can be done if your word processing program stores the report as an ASCII file (which all popular word processing programs do). You also can give someone the report stored on a disk. Even if the recipient uses a different word processing program, your report can be converted, read, changed, and even sent back to you. The person may also be able to incorporate your report into other ASCII programs, such as spreadsheet and desktop publishing programs.

Using ASCII You do not have to concern yourself with entering the proper code for conventional ASCII (0 to 127). This process occurs automatically as you type a character, press a command key such as the TAB key, or carry out other commands described in your program manual.

Program manuals generally explain how to enter ASCII codes 128 to 255. For example, a word processing program may tell you that to produce the Greek character π (pi) you have to:

> **type p**
> **press the ACCENT key**
> **type /**

Other programs may ask you to look up the actual code for the character, then type it into the computer, perhaps by activating and using the numeric keypad.

EXAMPLES OF ASCII CODES*

Some versions of ASCII, as shown here, use seven bits to represent characters 000 through 127. Other versions use eight bits, with the eighth bit called a parity bit. It is used for error-checking purposes, to help the computer determine whether the right number of bits were recorded.

SYMBOL	ASCII CODE	BINARY EQUIVALENT	SYMBOL	ASCII CODE	BINARY EQUIVALENT
%	037	0100101	A	065	1000001
&	038	0100110	B	066	1000010
0	048	0110000	C	067	1000011
1	049	0110001	D	068	1000100
2	050	0110010	a	097	1100001
3	051	0110011	b	098	1100010
:	058	0111010	c	099	1100011
;	059	0111011	d	100	1100100

* Check your computer and software manuals for listings of the complete ASCII code.

KINDS OF COMPUTERS

Some computers are special-purpose, or dedicated, computers. They are permanently programmed to handle one particular kind of task, such as studying weather phenomena. Embedded computers — for example, those found in thermostats, automobiles, and microwave ovens — are dedicated computers.

Most computers are general-purpose machines. They can handle many different kinds of tasks. To switch from one task to another, a user simply loads in a different program. This book is about general-purpose microcomputers.

Microcomputers

The vast majority of computers in use today are microcomputers. They also are called personal computers (pc's), because they are designed to be used by one person at a time. In microcomputers, the complete central processing unit (CPU) is assembled on a single silicon chip, called the microprocessor.

Manufacturers are building ever-smaller microcomputers. Today, the hundreds of different models are often categorized according to size:

- Desktop computers are microcomputers that are small enough to sit on the top of a desk.
- Laptop computers are small and light enough to be comfortably operated on a user's lap. They usually weigh between 8 and 12 pounds.
- Notebook computers typically weigh between 4 and 8 pounds.
- Subnotebook computers are similar to notebook computers but weigh even less.
- Palmtop computers weigh only about a pound and are small enough to be held in the palm of your hand. Yet they have many of the capabilities of a desktop computer.

As microcomputers have become more powerful and less costly, they have taken over many tasks formerly handled by larger computers. This trend has accelerated as the computer industry has improved the ability to connect microcomputers in networks with other microcomputers (and with larger computers).

Workstations These are high-performance microcomputers that are specialized for use in a particular field, such as engineering or graphics. ("Workstation" also has another meaning: a microcomputer connected to other microcomputers, or workstations, in a local area network.)

Minicomputers

Minicomputers are not much larger than desktop microcomputers. But they are more powerful and they are designed to be used by more than one person at a time. For example, all the cash registers in a supermarket may be connected to a minicomputer. The minicomputer stores information on all the sales rung up by the cash registers, and it keeps track of the supermarket's inventory of thousands of different products.

Mainframe Computers

Mainframes are large, powerful, expensive computers that may fill entire rooms, with CPUs as big as refrigerators. They are used mainly by government agencies, scientific research groups, and businesses such as banks, stock markets, and airlines, which must be able to process enormous amounts of data.

Supercomputers

Supercomputers are the fastest, most powerful, and most expensive computers. They are designed to tackle complex problems requiring vast amounts of computer time. For example, supercomputers are used to simulate extremely complex flight and weather phenomena; design airplanes, bridges, and medical drugs; conduct weapons research; and create special effects for motion pictures.

There are two types of supercomputers. Traditional supercomputers have one or several extremely complex and expensive processors and carry out computations serially, one at a time. Although able to carry out millions of operations per second, they are being succeeded by massively parallel supercomputers, which have thousands of simple, inexpensive processors connected in parallel. In a massively parallel system, a computational problem is divided into parts, with portions assigned simultaneously to various processors. The individual processors calculate subtotals and return them to a central processor for combining.

Like minicomputers and mainframes, supercomputers face competition from smaller computers. For example, scientists at Yale University created an inexpensive supercomputer by linking together 40 workstations scattered throughout the school's computer-science department. The scientists were able to produce a complex color image from a mathematical formula in seven minutes. It took ten times as long to complete the task on a $15 million supercomputer — and four hours to compute the image on a single workstation.

DIGITAL VERSUS ANALOG

Microcomputers and most larger computers are *digital computers*, so named because everything they do is translated into a series of numerals, or digits. But there's another kind of computer called an *analog computer*. Instead of processing discrete numbers, it measures the quantity of something that changes continuously, such as temperature or voltage. A good analogy is seen by comparing two kinds of clocks. A digital clock shows time as a series of minutes, jumping from 1:01 to 1:02 to 1:03, and so on. A more traditional clock has hands that sweep around the face, moving continuously and smoothly with the passage of time. Analog computers are used mainly in technical fields, such as engineering and weather prediction.

Chapter Two

COMPUTER HARDWARE

You can choose among many brands and models of microcomputers, or personal computers (pc's). But regardless of which computer you buy, you'll need the four basic kinds of hardware described in the previous chapter:

- Processing hardware: the central processing unit (CPU) and related hardware
- Input hardware: devices to enter information and instructions into the computer
- Output hardware: devices that receive information from the computer
- Storage hardware: devices that store output for later use.

These four kinds of devices comprise the physical portion of a computer system — the "nuts and bolts" portion that you can see and touch. Remember, however, that for hardware to do any work, it must be brought to life by programs, or software, a topic that is discussed in the following chapter.

PROCESSING HARDWARE

If you open up a pc, the most important item you'll see is the motherboard. It is a thin plastic circuit board fastened to the floor of the unit. Mounted on the motherboard is the microprocessor, or central processing unit (CPU), that is the computer's "brain." The *motherboard* also contains a number of other chips, such as memory chips, math chips, timing chips, and controller chips. Metallic tracks printed on the board comprise the electric circuitry that connects the chips.

It's the microprocessor that is of particular importance to you, the user. It plays a central role in determining how much work your computer system can do and how quickly it can perform that work. The microprocessor is the most important feature that distinguishes one computer from another.

Microprocessors

A microprocessor, like any other computer chip, is laden with microscopic transistors and other devices that act as on-off switches. Microscopic electrical pathways connect, or "integrate," the devices — hence the term integrated circuit. The greater the number of components in a microprocessor, the faster it can operate.

Each model of microprocessor is designed to perform certain specific functions. It contains permanent instructions and can also follow instructions in the software you use.

Microprocessor families   The two most widely used families of microprocessor chips are produced by Intel and Motorola. Intel chips are used by IBM PCs and manufacturers who build computers that are compatible with IBM PCs. Motorola chips are used in Apple and Apple Macintosh computers.

In both the Intel and Motorola microprocessor families, the earliest chips have the lowest model numbers; more recently introduced chips have higher model numbers. Each generation contains more transistors and other components, and thus is faster and more powerful than its predecessor. For example, Intel's 80386 chip is faster than its 80286 chip. (Note: Intel chip names are often abbreviated, with the 80386 simply called the 386, and the 80286 called the 286.)

The very first microprocessor, introduced in 1971, was the Intel 4004. It had 2,250 transistors. In 1993, Intel introduced the Pentium. It contains 3.1 million transistors — all on a square of silicon no bigger than the nail on one of your fingers.

Word size   One way to compare the power of microprocessors is to compare the number of bits they process at one time. This is called word size. The larger the word size, the more powerful and faster the microprocessor. At present, microprocessors for pc's fall into three categories:

- An 8-bit processor handles an 8-bit word
- A 16-bit processor handles a 16-bit word
- A 32-bit processor handles a 32-bit word.

Comparing Computer Speeds

Ever since computers were first invented, developers have raced to build ever faster machines. The earliest machines, in the late 1930s and early 1940s, could perform a few additions per second. Today's most powerful computers can perform billions of additions per second. There are two main reasons for this emphasis on speed:

1. Faster computers enable us to boost productivity and accomplish tasks more efficiently. Instead of spending an entire day calculating your taxes, it may take less than an hour when you use a tax program.

2. Faster computers enable us to do things that previously would have been impossible or impractical. Without computers, it would be too costly for company executives to expect fiscal statements from their accounting departments more than once a month. With computers, such statements are easily available on a daily basis.

Various methods can be used to measure and compare how fast CPUs compute. The measurement of primary importance to most microcomputer users is *megahertz*. Two other measurements you may hear are *mips* and *FLOPS*.

Megahertz If you're in the market for a microcomputer, you'll see models described as 16MHz or 25MHz or 66MHz. This measurement — megahertz (MHz) — indicates the *clock rate* of the CPU. One MHz equals one million electrical cycles per second.

A CPU contains a quartz clock that vibrates at a fixed speed. This regulates the rate at which pulses of electricity travel around the computer. The faster the clock vibrates, the higher the clock rate, and the faster the CPU can execute instructions. Thus a 66MHz computer is faster than a 50MHz computer — and much, much faster than a 16MHz computer.

What do these speeds mean in human terms? According to Intel, if the pulse of a 33MHz 80386 processor were slowed to the rate of a human heartbeat, it would take the processor a year to do the work that it normally accomplishes in one second!

Manufacturers may make different versions of the same micro-processor, with each running at different speeds. For example, Intel's 80486SX chip is available in 16MHz, 20MHz, and 25MHz versions. The 25MHz version has the highest price tag. However, while it offers a 25 percent performance increase over a 20MHz version, it may cost only 4 percent more.

Mips   Mips, or millions of instructions per second, indicates the number of instructions actually processed by a CPU within a period of time. Intel's 25MHz 80486SL microprocessor operates at 11 mips; a 33MHz version operates at 14.5 mips. In contrast, mainframes may work at the 70 to 80 mips level. And some super-computers are capable of processing over a billion instructions per second, giving rise to the acronym *gips* ("giga" means billion).

FLOPS   Perhaps the most widely accepted benchmark for measuring computer speed is FLOPS, or floating point operations per second. Floating point arithmetic is a method of calculating numbers in which the position of the decimal point is not fixed, but "floats." Each number is represented by a fixed part and an exponent — for example, 8.593×10^7.

Here's a comparison of FLOP speeds of several computers:

MICROCOMPUTERS

IBM PS/2-70	150,000 FLOPS
Macintosh IIfx	230,000 FLOPS

WORKSTATIONS

NeXT Cube	1,400,000 FLOPS
Sun Sparcstation	1,600,000 FLOPS

SUPERCOMPUTERS

NEC SX-3/12	4,231,000,000 FLOPS
Intel Touchstone Delta	8,600,000,000 FLOPS

If you keep up-to-date with developments in computer technology, you'll occasionally see the term *megaflop (Mflop)*. It equals one million FLOPS. For example, the Intel Touchstone Delta operates at a speed of 8,600 Mflops. Developers hope soon to have computers capable of *teraflops*, or trillions of calculations per second.

WIDELY USED MICROPROCESSORS

PRODUCT	USED IN	TYPICAL SPEEDS
8-bit microprocessors		
Intel 8088	IBM PC + compatibles	4.5 to 6 MHz
MOS 6502	Apple II, Atari 800, Commodore PET	1 to 2 MHz
Zilog Z80	TRS-80, ColecoVision	2 to 8 MHz
16-bit microprocessors		
Intel 80286	IBM PC/AT + compatibles	6 to 16 MHz
Motorola 68000	Apple II, Macintosh SE, Atari ST	8 to 16 MHz
32-bit microprocessors		
Intel 80386	IBM PS/2 + compatibles	16 to 40 MHz
Intel 80486	IBM PS/2 + compatibles	25 to 66 MHz
Motorola 68020	Macintosh II	16 to 20 MHz
Motorola 68030	NeXT, Macintosh IIsi	16 to 33 MHz
Motorola 68040	Macintosh Quadra	25 to 33 MHz

MEMORY

If you regularly ask your child to go to a grocery store, you do not have to tell the child each time how to leave your home, which path to take to the store, how to enter the store, where to find the milk, how to pick up the milk, where to take the milk, how to pay for it, and so on. The child's memory handles all these aspects of the task. Without memory, a human would be virtually helpless.

A computer's central processing unit (CPU) is equally dependent on memory. If a computer had no memory, you would have to feed every instruction into the CPU each time you asked it to perform a task. This is exactly what had to be done with the earliest computers; even the simplest instructions had to be read into the machine from special punch cards or tape.

Residing within the computer are two types of internal memory: ROM and RAM.

Read-Only Memory (ROM)

Read-only memory (ROM) contains a built-in set of instructions needed by the computer. The computer cannot change or add to these instructions; it can only "read" the instructions. Material in ROM is permanent; it is not lost when the computer is turned off.

Different kinds of computers store different kinds of instructions in ROM. But some instructions are needed by all computers. For example, all computers need instructions that tell them how to display text on the display screen.

Part of ROM is used by BIOS — the Basic Input/Output System. BIOS is a series of programs that facilitate input and output operations, such as transferring data from the keyboard to the central processing unit (CPU) or from the CPU to the monitor, printer, or disk drive.

ROM also contains instructions that translate programs written in high-level languages into machine language, plus instructions on how to do mathematical computations. Usually, ROM also contains a diagnostic program that carries out a series of tests whenever the computer is turned on. The program's purpose is to determine if the system is functioning properly and if not, to locate the source of any problem.

Random-Access Memory (RAM)

Random-access memory (RAM) is used to store programs and data with which you currently are working, such as a game you're playing or a mailing list you're updating. RAM can be both "read" and "written to." It can be changed, erased, and added to. It's called random access because you can instantly go to any part of the memory. You do not have to go through all the data stored in RAM to reach the data you want.

RAM is temporary memory. Its contents are not permanent. When you turn off the computer, everything in RAM is erased. Any changes you made (such as additions to that mailing list) are lost forever — unless you copied, or saved, the data onto disks or other storage media before you turned off the computer.

RAM is what's usually referred to when someone talks about computer memory. If you hear that a computer has 640K of internal memory, it means that it has 640 kilobytes of RAM. Not too many years ago, 640K of RAM was a lot. Today, many pc's come with 4MB (megabytes) or more of RAM.

The larger the capacity of RAM — that is, the greater the number of bytes it can hold — the more efficient the computer. Before the CPU can process data or execute an instruction, the information must be in RAM. If it's on a disk, it must be located and transferred into RAM, which takes time. Thus, for example, a spreadsheet program will perform much better if an entire spreadsheet can fit in RAM than if parts of the spreadsheet must be transferred in from a disk.

Also, computers with lots of RAM can run bigger, more complex programs than computers with little RAM. A computer with only 256K of RAM cannot run a program that requires 640K of RAM. (The RAM requirements of a commercial software package are printed on the box.)

You can increase the amount of RAM on your system by plugging a memory board into a slot inside the computer. For example, a computer with 4MB of RAM may be expandable to 64MB.

Want to know how much memory your system has? Check the documentation that came with your computer and with any memory boards that you installed.

On IBM and IBM-compatible computers, there may be as many as three different kinds of RAM, which makes things rather confusing:

Conventional RAM is the first 640K of RAM. Most computers have at least 256K of conventional memory. A significant portion is used up by the operating system. Whatever is left over is available for running programs.

Extended RAM is memory above 640K on computers with 80286, 80386, and 80486 microprocessors. Many of these machines are sold with a total of 1MB of RAM.

To use extended memory efficiently, you need to install a special program called an extended memory manager. This program "manages" the memory, making sure that several programs do not try to use the same memory at the same time. (Commercial programs that use extended RAM often come with their own extended memory manager.)

Expanded RAM is another kind of RAM above 640K. It can be added to almost any pc model. To use expanded memory, you need to install a special program called an expanded memory manager, which is sold with the expanded memory board. The program allows your application programs to access the expanded RAM.

INPUT DEVICES

When you work with a computer, you are constantly giving it instructions and information. For instance, if you are playing a shoot-em-up space game, you have to tell the computer how to move your spaceship and when to fire rockets at the enemy. If you are designing a home, you have to tell the computer how large each room should be and where to put doors. To communicate such information, you use an input device.

You can't just plug an input device into a computer and expect to use it. The computer also has to be given instructions on how to use the device. Instructions on how to use a keyboard usually are built into a computer's operating system. Instructions for using a mouse may be part of the operating system or you may have to load special software. Other input devices generally must be used with software that contains the necessary instructions. For example, most game software contains instructions that tell the computer how to work with a joystick.

Keyboards

Keyboards are the most widely used input devices. Each time you press a key on a keyboard, you send an instruction to the central processing unit (CPU). Exactly what instruction you send depends on the specific key and on the software you are using.

A computer keyboard looks very much like a traditional typewriter keyboard. One major difference is that the computer keyboard contains a variety of additional keys that enable you to do much more with the computer than you can with a typewriter. Another important difference is that it's a lot easier to correct mistakes on a computer than on a typewriter; if you press the D key when you meant to press the S key, simply press the Back Space key and the D is erased.

Pressing a letter or a number key by itself sends the instruction to display the letter or number. This is true with all computer keyboards. But exactly what happens when you press some of the other keys depends on the software, which means that you often have to learn different commands to use with different programs. For example, pressing the F1 key while you're using a spreadsheet program may display a graph, but pressing F1 in your word processing program may display a list of command options.

Often, you have to hold down two or more keys at the same time. For example, to type *Hello* you have to simultaneously hold down the H key and a Shift Key to make the capital H. Many commands are given to the computer using a combination of special keys. For example, a word processing program may switch to **bold face** type when you press the Alt-B combination.

Here's a rundown of keys found on most keyboards:

QWERTY keys Letters of the alphabet are arranged in the same way on almost all computer and typewriter keyboards. This is called a QWERTY arrangement (pronounced "kwerty"), a name derived from the first six letters on the top alphabetic row.

Number keys The numerals 1 through 0 are arranged in a row above the QWERTY keys. As on a typewriter keyboard, pressing one of these keys simultaneously with a SHIFT key produces the character shown above the number on the key.

A TYPICAL KEYBOARD

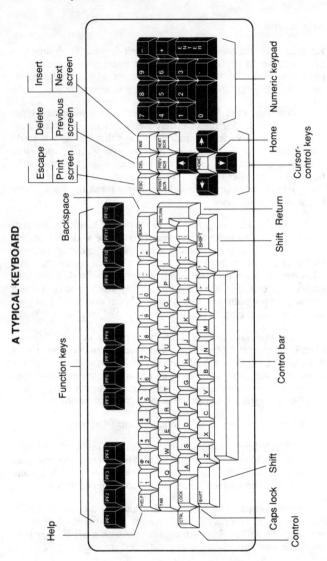

Arrow keys   Four keys marked with arrows control movement of the cursor. This is the small spot of light on the display screen that indicates where data are to be entered or erased. One arrow points up, one down, one right, and one left. The direction indicates in which direction the key moves the cursor.

Command keys   Arrow keys are examples of command keys. They do not instruct the computer to produce a character. Instead, they instruct the computer to take a certain action. Other command keys include:

ENTER: Called RETURN on some computers, this key usually is marked with a bent, left-pointing arrow. It has various uses. For example, in word processing, pressing ENTER moves the cursor to the beginning of the next line. Often, after entering a command, you have to press ENTER to tell the computer to execute the command.

SHIFT: These two keys are used to make letters uppercase and to enter certain punctuation marks and other characters. They have additional functions in some application programs.

CAPS LOCK: This is an example of a toggle key. By pressing it, you can switch back and forth ("toggle") between two modes. The first time you press Caps Lock, all succeeding letters that you type will be uppercase. The next time you press Caps Lock, you return to lowercase letters.

TAB: Pressing Tab jumps the cursor to the next tab stop on the display screen. Many programs allow you to customize the location of tab stops. This is useful for such tasks as creating tables containing several columns of figures.

CONTROL (Ctrl): When pressed simultaneously with one or more additional keys, Ctrl performs a program command. For example, in some word processing programs, pressing Ctrl and A moves the cursor left one word.

ALTERNATE FUNCTION (Alt): Like Ctrl, Alt is used in combination with other keys to perform program commands.

BACK SPACE: Marked with a straight left-pointing arrow, it moves the cursor one position to the left.

ESCAPE (Esc): This key is defined in various ways by different software. For example, in a game, pressing ESCAPE may allow you to pause, or "freeze" the game.

Function keys Keys numbered F1 through F10 or even higher are used by application programs for specific purposes, or functions. For example, a word processing program may assign the command "save this file" to the F3 key when F3 is pressed after F1.

Numeric keypad Some computers have a numeric keypad located to one side of the keyboard. It looks very much like the keys of a pocket calculator, and it serves the same purpose: to enter numbers into a program. The numeric keypad is turned on and off by pressing the Num Lock key above the keypad. When the keypad is "on," it can be used to enter numbers. When it is "off," its keys can be used to move the cursor.

Mice

Computers have given the word *mouse* a new meaning. When people say "I played with my mouse," you must wonder if they're talking about a live pet or a small box attached to their computer. Most people would agree, however, that the infestation of computer mice has been very beneficial, whereas a comparable invasion of live mice would not be welcome!

Computer mice are the most widely supported alternative to keyboards. That is, there's lots of business, educational, and other application software that works with mice. Instead of typing instructions to the computer, you use the mouse to point to commands on the display screen. Exactly what a mouse is used for depends on the application program. Generally, however, mice can be used to:

- Open and close menus
- Choose a menu option
- Start a program or move from one program to another
- Select, open, close, move, or resize a window on the screen
- Scroll through material in a window
- Select text within a document
- View the contents of a disk.

A mouse sits on the desk next to the computer. It has one or more buttons. As you move the mouse around, a cursor or pointer on the display screen also moves. Let's say you're working with your mailing list program and you want to print a list of names and addresses. You move the mouse until the cursor is on the PRINT command in the menu. (A menu is a list of options available to you.) You tell the computer you want this command by clicking (pressing and quickly releasing) one of the buttons on the mouse. The computer then executes your command. Some commands require that you double-click: when the cursor is on the desired object, you rapidly click the mouse button twice.

A mouse makes it easier and more inviting to use many programs. You do not have to memorize commands or look them up in a manual. It's called a *graphic user interface* as opposed to the *text-based user interface* of a keyboard. Macintosh computers and computers that work with Microsoft Windows are among those that use mice and graphic interfaces. Note, however, that you still need the keyboard to write text.

Most mice are connected to the computer by cable (the mouse's "tail"). Some mice are wireless; they work like television remote controls. People generally keep their mice on pads, though this is not always necessary. However, a pad protects your desktop and muffles noise.

How much work space is needed to move a mouse around depends on the mouse's resolution—that is, its ability to pinpoint a specific location on the display screen. The higher the resolution, the smaller the amount of space needed. Typical mouse resolutions range from 100 to 300 dots per inch.

Other Input Devices

Trackball   A trackball looks rather like a Ping-Pong ball set into a base. It serves the same purposes as a mouse but because it is stationary it requires much less space. It also requires less arm and wrist movement than a mouse. Many portable computers use built-in trackballs instead of mice.

To move the cursor or pointer on the screen, you roll the track-ball with your fingers or the palm of your hand. Some trackballs come with several buttons that have the same function as mouse buttons. Trackballs contain technology that emulates, or imitates, a mouse, so they can be used with any software designed to work with mice.

Stylus A pen-based computer uses a special pen-like stylus that takes letters and numbers written on the computer's flat screen and translates them into binary code. The stylus also can be used to make program choices by checking boxes on the screen — rather like filling out an electronic form. Material must be neatly printed for the computer to understand it.

ARE WE COMPATIBLE?

One of the most important questions you need to ask when buying hardware or software is, "Is it compatible with my computer?" That is, "Will it work with my computer?"

Compatibility requires standards. Manufacturers and technical organizations have established standards on a broad range of issues: how graphics are displayed on a monitor, how data is transmitted by modems, how messages should be transferred within a network, and so on. Some standards are accepted internationally; others are unique to a country or region, which can create problems for people who travel.

In order to use a printer or any other peripheral with a computer, the peripheral and the computer must be compatible. They must be able to use the same interface, or channel, to transmit data. Several standard interfaces exist. One standard interface is the Centronics parallel interface. Centronics interfaces are used to interface many printers to computers. If you have a printer with a Centronics interface but your computer requires the use of another type of interface, you may still be able to have the two devices work together, but you'll have to install a special interface board.

You may hear or see the term "plug compatible." Devices that are plug compatible can be plugged into the same interface sockets

However, as the technology becomes more sophisticated, these computers are expected to be able to decipher most people's handwriting.

Graphics (digitizing) tablets   These input devices use the same sensing technology used by pen-based computers, but they are designed primarily for drawing. They let you make sketches and highly detailed drawings, just as you would on a piece of paper. Indeed, they have a flat drawing surface similar to that of a pad, or tablet, of paper. Generally, you use a special pen to draw on the tablet's pressure-sensitive surface. The tablet's electronics

---

and used interchangeably, without modification within the computer system. For example, a Centronics and a Centronics-compatible printer are plug compatible, though their internal technology, capabilities, and costs may differ.

The type of microprocessor found in a computer determines what software can be used on the computer. The software has to be compatible with the microprocessor. Application software also has to be compatible with the operating system — which, in turn, has to be compatible with the microprocessor. Such information is typically printed on a product's packaging.

For example, a software package may state that the software is designed for "IBM PCs or compatibles with DOS2.0+." This tells you that you can use the software on an IBM PC or any computer that is compatible with the IBM PC, as long as the MS-DOS operating system, version 2.0 or higher, is installed in the computer. The software will not work on systems that do not meet these criteria.

Yet another term you'll hear is *clone*. This refers to a computer that is compatible to an IBM PC but made by another manufacturer. A clone can run software designed for use on an IBM PC. Among the many companies that make IBM clones are Compaq, Dell, Gateway, NEC, and Toshiba.

enable it to pinpoint the location of each point in your drawing. It translates this data into binary digits for the computer, which then presents an accurate image of your drawing on the display screen.

Graphics tablets are particularly useful for architects, graphic designers, engineers, and other people whose work involves some type of illustration. For example, let's say you have a blueprint on paper that you want to put into a drafting program you're using on the computer. Simply put the blueprint on top of the graphics tablet, tape it down so it doesn't move, and trace it. Once the blueprint has been entered into the program, you can quickly make — and unmake! — any number of changes in it.

Touch screens A pressure-sensitive display screen allows you to choose a menu option or function by pressing the screen at the appropriate place. Such screens are often used in public information systems and for training purposes. They have limited value for applications that require frequent input, because repeatedly touching the screen is tiring. Also, fingerprints tend to cloud the screens.

Light pen A light pen has light sensors in its tip, and is held like a regular pen. It is used to communicate with the computer via the display screen. You can use the pen to point to and choose a command shown on the screen. Or you can create a drawing by touching the screen at various points or by moving the pen across the screen; the computer translates the drawing into binary code and stores it. Light pens are not supported by large amounts of software. Like touch screens, using them for any length of time becomes tiring.

Joystick A joystick has a movable lever and one or more buttons. Joysticks are used mainly for games. As the lever is moved in various directions, it causes corresponding movements of an object on the screen. Pressing a button usually causes an action such as the firing of a weapon.

Optical scanners Scanners scan, or "read," text and pictures, converting them into electrical signals that are decoded into binary numbers, which are sent into the computer. A scanner that inputs only text is called an optical character reader (OCR). Printers and publishers are major users of optical scanners. Many other businesses have begun to use optical scanners in conjunction with desktop publishing programs, as they produce their own company newsletters, annual reports, manuals, and so on.

Bar code readers   Optical scanners called bar code readers are used to scan those little black-striped symbols found on everything from groceries to employee ID badges. The codes can appear in a variety of shapes and sizes, and may be accompanied by the decimal numbers they represent. Some codes are invisible to human eyes, but visible to the infrared radiation used by the scanning devices. There are several types of readers:

- Penlike devices known as wand readers that are swept across the surface of a bar code
- Gun readers, which use a beam of light to detect a code and do not actually touch the code
- Swipe readers designed to read bar codes on cards similar to credit cards.

Some models are connected to the computer either with an expansion card or via the connector normally used by the keyboard. Other models are stand-alone units; they do not have to be connected to the pc during data collection. They store the data until you connect them to your computer's serial port.

Organizations use bar codes for a broad range of functions: track inventory, compile workers' time and attendance records, route mail, check out library books, ensure that parts are fed into an assembly line in the correct sequence, control access to buildings, verify identities of hospital patients, etc.

Video digitizers   These devices enable you to change video images, such as those taken with a camcorder, into computer-readable form. The images can then be incorporated into newsletters and other computer-generated material. They also can be sent via modem to other computers. For example, a police department may use a video digitizer to enter scenes of a bank robbery or film of known criminals into the computer, then transmit this data to a computer in a distant police department.

Speech recognition devices   These devices enable computers to hear and record spoken words, and to respond to spoken commands. The spoken words are changed into binary code, then either matched with words stored in the computer's memory or broken down into phonemes (the sound building blocks of words). Speech recognition is extremely difficult because of the enormous differences in pitch and pronounciation among various speakers. Speech recognition devices are still in their infancy. However, they already have some applications and they certainly have great potential.

Musical keyboards A musical, or electronic, keyboard is an instrument that looks somewhat like a shortened piano keyboard, with buttons that enable it to mimic a host of instruments. Musical keyboards can be used on their own. Or, using a technology called Musical Instrument Digital Interface (MIDI), they can communicate with computers, thereby expanding their versatility. For example, with the appropriate software, you can use a musical keyboard to learn how to play a piano, or to compose, edit, and print songs.

OUTPUT DEVICES

As you work with a computer you want to see what you — and the computer! — are doing. You may also want to show other people the results of your labors. Just as there are a variety of ways to enter data into a computer, there are a number of ways to get data out of the computer.

Here, too, the computer needs instructions on how to use a particular output device. This may be handled by hardware, software, or a combination of the two.

Monitors

Monitors, the most common output devices, give nearly instantaneous display of a computer's output. A monitor is like a television set. Indeed, many early pc's used television sets as output devices; video game machines, which are a type of special-purpose computer, still connect to television sets to display their images.

Some computers, such as the Macintosh and all portable machines, have built-in display screens. Others work with monitors that are connected via cables.

Monitors display both text and graphics. A typical monitor can display 25 rows of text, each containing 80 characters (letters, numerals, etc.). The screens of some small computers, such as palmtops, cannot display as much material.

Types of displays Two types of display technologies are dominant in the pc industry: cathode ray tube and liquid crystal.

Cathode ray tubes (CRTs), with their TV-like screens, are the standard displays used in desktop monitors. Indeed, the term *CRT* is often used as a synonym for *monitor*. One disadvantage of CRTs is their bulk. Another disadvantage is the fact that CRTs emit low-level electromagnetic radiation, which has been implicated in health problems such as miscarriages, birth defects, and certain cancers, although scientists have not proven that monitor radiation actually causes these problems (see Chapter Six).

Liquid-crystal displays are used in the flat-panel displays of small computers such as laptops and notebooks. This technology uses comparatively little power and eliminates the bulk associated with CRTs.

Monochrome versus color One of the major differences among monitors is the number of colors they display.

Monochrome monitors display one-color (monochrome) images. Usually, the image is white, green, or amber, and the background is black.

Depending on the model, a color monitor can simultaneously display anywhere from 16 to thousands of colors. Color monitors are more expensive than monochrome monitors. They also tend to flicker more, which can increase the possibility of eyestrain when used over long periods of time.

Image sharpness and detail Images on a computer screen are made up of small dots of light called pixels or, less commonly, pels (both terms are shortened forms of "picture elements"). Every memory location on the screen — that is, every point on the screen that can be addressed by the computer — is represented by a pixel. The greater the number of memory locations, the greater the number of pixels, and the more detailed an image can be.

The sharpness of an image is called its resolution. Monitor resolution usually is expressed in the number of pixels horizontally times the number vertically. For example, a resolution of 640 x 480 means that there are 640 pixels in each horizontal row, and a total of 480 horizontal rows on the screen.

The higher the resolution, the more realistic and sharper the image. A tree drawn on a system with high resolution has a more natural, rounded shape than a tree drawn on a system with low resolution; the latter looks boxy, as if it were created by filling in boxes on a piece of graph paper. The difference is understandable when you realize that a monitor with a resolution of 320 x 200 has 64,000 pixels, while a monitor with a resolution of 640 x 480 has 307,200 pixels. Comparing the images that can be created on these monitors is like comparing the images you could create by filling in the squares in graph paper with 1-inch squares and graph paper with ½-inch squares.

High-resolution ("high-res") color graphics is critical in many fields, including CAD/CAM (computer-aided design and computer-aided manufacturing), architectural engineering, and desktop publishing. It's also needed for many games and is preferred for windowing environments, such as Microsoft *Windows*.

Resolution depends on two pieces of hardware: the monitor, which must have a high-enough density of pixels to provide the resolution you want, and the graphics adapter card.

Graphics adapter card   In order to display material on the screen, a computer needs a graphics adapter card (also called a display adapter card). This is a special circuit board installed either directly on the motherboard or in an expansion slot. It takes the video instructions from the software you are using and translates them into signals that can be understood by the monitor. It tells the monitor which pixels are to be lighted and which colors are to be used.

Of course, the monitor has to have the ability to follow the instructions it receives. For example, a color graphics adapter card cannot function with a monochrome monitor.

Software also has certain requirements or preferred combinations of monitor and card. Microsoft Windows can be used with a

GRAPHICS STANDARDS

Six graphics adapters have dominated the IBM PC and compatibles market since IBM introduced its first pc in 1981:

MDA (Monochrome Display Adapter): the monochrome display on the original IBM PC, capable of displaying text but no graphics; now obsolete.

HGC (Hercules Graphics Card): provides a high-quality monochrome display of both text and graphics.

CGA (Color/Graphics Adapter): the first color display adapter for pc's; displayed two colors in a resolution of 640 x 200 and four colors at 320 x 200; the poor resolution resulted in very fuzzy text; now obsolete.

EGA (Enhanced Graphics Adapter): the successor to CGA, with improved resolution (640 x 350) and the ability to display up to 16 colors; now obsolete.

VGA (Video Graphics Array): provides a resolution of 640 x 480 and displays as many as 256 colors simultaneously from a palette of 256,000 colors; has replaced CGA and EGA as the graphics standard.

SVGA (Super VGA): An enhanced version of VGA; provides a resolution of up to 1064 x 768 and better 256-color graphics.

monochrome monitor and a monochrome card, but its capabilities are best exploited on a high-resolution color monitor with a super-video graphics array card.

Printers

Much of the work you do on a computer wouldn't be as useful if you couldn't produce printed copies of the work. When writing a report on the computer, you want to be able to print it so you can give it to your teacher or employer. When preparing bills for clients, you want to make paper copies of the bills. When discussing a project with employees, you may want to provide them with graphs showing the timing of each task in the project. When calling on customers, you may want to take along printouts of the customers' sales records.

The printed output of a computer is called a *printout* or *hard copy* (as opposed to the *soft copy* that appears on the display screen and is easily changed, replaced, or erased).

Major types of printers   Printers are classified in one of two groups:

- Impact printers include dot matrix and daisy-wheel printers. They form images in the same manner as an ordinary typewriter: a print head strikes an inked ribbon, causing ink to be transferred onto paper.

- Non-impact printers include laser, thermal, and ink-jet printers. They form images by spraying or fusing ink onto paper. They are much faster and quieter than impact printers and produce higher quality copy. They cost more than impact printers, though prices have fallen sharply in recent years.

Dot matrix printer   These printers form characters from a matrix pattern of tiny dots. Each dot is made by a pin striking an inked ribbon and pushing it against the paper. There are two kinds of dot matrix printers: the original 9-pin models and the more advanced 24-pin models. The latter can be set to work at two speeds: a very high speed for *draft quality* output and a somewhat slower speed for better *near-letter quality* output.

Dot matrix printers are widely used in homes, offices, and schools. Most portable printers also are dot-matrix machines. Dot-matrix printers are fast, durable, and inexpensive. They can print both text and graphics, and they can print multipart forms such as those used for invoices. However, they are noisy and their print quality is inferior to that produced by other types of printers.

Daisy-wheel printers   A daisy-wheel printer has a circular printing element composed of a series of spokes, or "petals," each of which contains molded characters. The printing element rotates until the desired character is in position to be struck by a hammer.

A DOT MATRIX CHARACTER

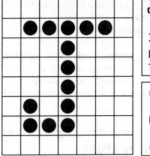

draft

In draft mode, a 24—
printer produces typ
type produced by a 9-

near-letter quality

Most 24-pin dot matrix pr
type, producing text that
similar to text produced

Daisy-wheel printers produce letter-quality copy and are often referred to as *letter-quality printers*. However, they are slow and noisy, and they cannot print graphics. They now are largely obsolete.

Laser printers These printers use the same technology as a photocopy machine. A laser forms images of text and other data on a light-sensitive, rotating drum. Dry ink, or toner, is attracted to the images and then transferred onto paper.

Laser printers generate exceptionally fine, high-resolution copy. First-generation models print at 300 dots per inch (the equivalent of 90,0000 dots per square inch); newer models are capable of printing 600 dots per inch. Laser printers operate quietly and quickly, and can print text, graphics, and colors.

As prices have fallen, laser printers have become increasingly popular, though they still cost significantly more than dot matrix printers. They also are costlier to maintain. They are large machines, and can be very sensitive to dust, humidity, and other environmental factors.

Thermal printers These printers use heated styluses to burn characters and graphic images onto special heat-sensitive paper. They produce good-quality output; print text, graphics, and colors; and are fast and quiet. But their high cost and need for special paper are drawbacks.

Ink-jet printers These printers form images by spraying very fine jets of ink from tiny nozzles directly onto paper. Each ink droplet has about one-millionth the volume of a drop of water from an eyedropper. Indeed, like laser printers, some 90,000 dots may be placed in a square inch of paper, each one positioned perfectly!

Ink-jet printers are small; quiet; and can print text, graphics, and colors. The print quality is often comparable to that of laser printers — in fact, some models are advertised as *laser-quality printers*. However, they're much slower than laser printers and the

BASIC PRINTER FEATURES

Print quality Refers to the resolution, or sharpness of the printed images. Print quality is measured in dots per inch (dpi) — the higher the dpi, the better the resolution and, not surprisingly, the higher the cost

Typeface Refers to the distinctive design of a set of type. Some printers have only one or two typefaces built in, with all type printed in the same size. At the other extreme are laser printers that have a generous assortment of built-in fonts scalable to virtually any size. Many printers allow users to add additional typefaces either through plug-in cartridges or by downloading them from software.

Black versus color The most popular printers print in black only — their popularity probably stemming from the fact that most people's computer output consists of text. Models that can print in color are expensive, especially those that produce high-resolution output. They also are notoriously slow.

Memory Refers to the amount of built-in random-access memory (RAM) in the printer. More RAM means higher speeds, sharper graphics, and the ability to store more typefaces.

Carriage width Indicates the paper width that the printer can accommodate. A 9½- or 10-inch carriage width handles ordinary ink must be given time to dry in order to avoid smearing. Purchase and maintenance costs fall between those of dot-matrix and laser models.

Plotters

Like a printer, a plotter produces hard copy. But instead of printing text, it uses pens to draw graphs, diagrams, and pictures. Plotters are particularly useful to architects, interior decorators, engineers, mathematicians, and other people who make heavy use

---

paper used for correspondence, reports, etc. Applications such as spreadsheets generally require a carriage that can handle paper up to 15 inches wide.

Paper feed   Paper can be fed into an impact printer either one sheet at a time or on a continuous roll. The latter requires a device called a tractor, which has sprockets that fit into pre-punched holes on the right and left edges of the paper. Some printers can print labels and envelops; others do not have this capability.

Speed   Indicates how quickly the printer produces a finished page. The speed of dot matrix printers is measured in characters per second (cps). Laser printers are rated in pages per minute (ppm). While useful for comparison purposes, speeds provided by manufacturers often are higher than those actually experienced by users. For example, printing graphics takes much longer than printing text; dot-matrix printing in near-letter-quality mode takes longer than printing in draft mode.

Buffer   A printer buffer consists of extra memory, either within the printer or in a separate unit between the printer and the computer. The computer loads the document into the buffer, from which it is fed into the printer (which operates more slowly than the computer). The larger the buffer, the larger the document it can hold. The buffer frees the computer so that it can be used for other tasks while the document is being printed.

of graphics in their work. Small, low-cost desktop plotters also are finding wide application among businesses that wish to produce color slides and overhead transparencies for presentations.

A plotter has one or more pens that move over paper on a flat bed. Exactly where each pen moves and draws is determined by instructions from the software. The finer the increments in which the pens move, the higher the plotter's resolution. The speed at which a plotter works is measured in inches per second (ips); pens of typical desktop plotters may plot at speeds of 12 inches per second.

The number of pen colors ranges from one to twenty or more, depending on the plotter model. Water-based ink is used for plotting on paper; oil-based ink is used for making slides and overhead transparencies.

Modems

A modem actually is an input-output device. It lets a computer send and receive data via ordinary telephone lines — just like a telephone lets you converse with people at the other end of telephone lines.

The term *modem* is an acronym for modulator-demodulator. As shown in the illustration, a modem converts digital signals (electric pulses representing binary 1s and 0s) generated by the computer into analog signals (tones) for transmission. A modem at the other end of the telephone line receives the analog signals and converts them back into digital signals that its computer can understand.

Communications software   To enable a computer, modem, and telephone to work together, you need communications software. Many modems are sold with the software they need. Some on-line services require you to use communications programs designed especially for their systems.

External and internal modems   Modems are either external or internal. An external modem is a separate unit, with its own power supply. It is attached to the computer with a cable. An internal modem is a printed circuit board that you install in a slot inside your computer.

USING A MODEM

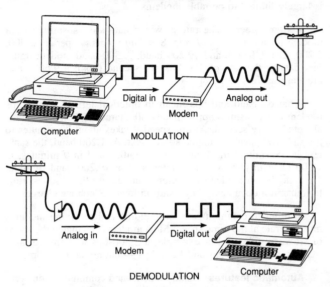

Digital in — Modem — Analog out

MODULATION

Computer

Analog in — Modem — Digital out

DEMODULATION

Computer

An external modem has a panel with a series of status indicator lights, which tell you what's happening in the communication process. For example:

- The carrier detect (CD) indicator lights up when the modem makes contact with another modem.
- The send data (SD) indicator flashes each time a byte of data passes through the modem from the computer to the telephone line.
- The receive data (RD) indicator flashes each time an incoming byte of data passes through the modem.

Most external modems are shaped like flat boxes and are plugged directly into the phone line. Acoustic couplers are a type of external modem that work through a telephone handset. You place the phone into two rubber cups on the acoustic coupler; data from your computer goes out through the phone's mouthpiece and incoming data is received via the phone's earpiece. Originally, all external modems were acoustic couplers. Today, this technology is largely limited to portable modems.

Modem speed The rate at which data are transmitted by a modem is called the *baud rate*. Standard modems operate at 300, 1,200, 2,400, 9,600, and 19,200 baud. A 300-baud modem transfers data at the rate of 300 bits per second (bps); a 9,600-baud modem transfers 9,600 bps.

What do baud and bps mean in practical terms? A 300-bps modem can transmit approximately 30 characters (letters, numerals, etc.) every second. At this speed it takes about 72 minutes to transmit 100 pages of double-spaced text. At 1,200 baud, the same text is transmitted in 18 minutes; at 2,400 baud in 9 minutes; at 9,600 baud in just over 2 minutes; and at 19,200 baud in about 1 minute. Faster modems cost more, but because they use less time to transmit a document, they result in lower telephone charges.

In order to communicate, the sending and receiving modems must operate at the same speed. Most modems can match the speed of slower modems. For example, a 2,400-bps modem can also transmit data at 300 bps and 1,200 bps — but not at 9,600 bps.

Automatic features Some modems and communications programs offer handy automatic capabilities, including:

- Auto-dialer: the modem automatically dials a telephone number typed into the communications program.
- Auto-redial: the modem automatically redials a telephone number until a connection is made.
- Auto-answer: the modem automatically "picks up" after a programmed number of rings.
- Automatic voice/data switching: the modem allows a person to break into the middle of a data transmission to speak on the telephone.

STORAGE DEVICES

Like modems, storage devices can be thought of as combination input-output devices. Storage devices hold, or store, programs and data sent to them by a computer so that the material can be sent back to a computer at some future time. Floppy and hard disks are the most common storage media, but magnetic tape and CD-ROM also are popular.

The amount of data that can be stored on a storage device is measured in kilobytes (K) and megabytes (MB). The more information a device can hold, the more convenient it is to use. For example, a 1.44MB disk holds about twice as much data as a 720K disk. Using ten 1.44MB disks to hold all your data instead of twenty 720K disks means:

- Fewer disks to keep track of
- The ability to store larger files (instead of having to break up a large file, such as a long mailing list, into two smaller files)
- Less need to spend time switching back and forth between disks.

Floppy Disk Drives

One of the most common storage devices used with pc's is the floppy disk — also called a *diskette*, or just plain *floppy*. Data is stored on the disk's special magnetic coating.

Floppy disks come in two sizes. Those that are 5¼ inches wide are made of thin plastic and are flexible, hence the origin of the name. Those that are 3½ inches wide have rigid plastic cases. They are sometimes called *microdisks* or *microfloppies*.

- 5¼-inch disks hold 180K (single-density disks, now obsolete), 360K (double-density disks), or 1.2MB (high-density disks) of data.
- 3½-inch disks hold either 720K (double-density) or 1.4MB (high-density).

In order for a computer to write information onto a disk or read information from a disk, the disk must be placed in a device called a disk drive. The drive may be built into the computer, or it may be a separate unit.

The disk drive spins the disk at a very high speed. A mechanism called the read/write head moves over the surface of the disk, separated from the disk by a very thin layer of air. The head either reads or writes data, depending on instructions it receives from the software being run on the computer.

**FLOPPY
  DISKS**

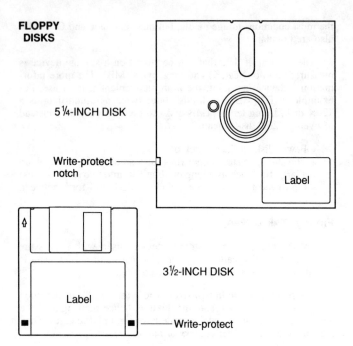

5¼-INCH DISK

Write-protect
notch

Label

3½-INCH DISK

Label

Write-protect

Each drive is designed to be used with a specific size and density of floppy disk. However, drives designed to handle higher-density disks can also use lower-density disks of the same size. Thus a 1.4MB 3½-inch drive can read a 720K 3½-inch disk. But a 720K drive cannot read a 1.4MB disk.

Some pc's contain both 5¼-inch and 3½-inch drives. Desktop pc's often have room for two floppy disk drives, even though they may be sold with only one drive. It's relatively easy for a user to install a second drive should the need arise. Let's say your desktop computer has a 5¼-inch drive but you've just bought a notebook computer with a 3½-inch drive. Installing a 3½-inch drive into the desktop model enables you do move disks from one computer to the other. An alternative, of course, is to use an external 3½-inch drive.

Hard Disk Drives

Most pc's sold today have a built-in hard disk drive in addition to one or two floppy disk drives. You'll want at least one floppy drive even if you have a hard disk drive, because software is sold on floppies. In some cases, you then run the software from the floppies or you can install it on your hard disk. However, many of today's most popular application programs require a hard disk because they take up more megabytes than are available on a floppy.

Hard drives cost more than floppy drives but they offer two big advantages: speed and high storage capacity.

- The amount of time needed for a disk drive to find and retrieve data is called the access time. The average access time for a 140MB drive is 18 milliseconds (ms); for a 40MB drive it's 28 ms; for a 1.44MB floppy it's 200 ms.
- Many computers are now sold with 40MB, 60MB, 80MB and 140MB hard drives, and even higher-capacity drives are available. A 60MB drive can hold the equivalent of 15,000 typed pages of double-spaced text!

A hard disk and its drive are permanently sealed in a metal box. There are one or more rigid, magnetically coated platters stacked on a spindle. As the spindle spins the platters at speeds up to 6,000 revolutions per minute, read/write heads skim over each platter surface, reading or recording data in response to software commands.

Magnetic Tape

Magnetic tape systems are used mainly by businesses as a form of backup. That is, people use them to store duplicate ("backup") copies of data on their hard disks, in case something goes wrong with the disks.

Backing up data on magnetic tape is much faster and less error-prone than backing up on floppies. Also, a single magnetic tape cartridge can store 200MB or more. In other words, you can store the entire contents of your hard drive on one cartridge!

Magnetic tape has one big disadvantage, which precludes it from replacing floppies for uses other than backup storage: it stores data sequentially, one bit after another. To find a particular file, you must read through every item that precedes it on the tape (though you can fast-forward). In contrast, a disk offers random access; data can be retrieved more or less equally rapidly from anywhere on the disk's surface.

Tape cartridges fit into a device called a tape backup unit. Both internal and external units are available.

CD-ROM

The same compact disks that have revolutionized the recording industry can be used to store computer data. CD-ROM stands for *compact disk — read only memory*. Information stored on CD-ROM disks by the manufacturer can be read by your computer. But you cannot erase this information. Nor can you record your own data on the disks.

To use CD-ROM disks, you need to connect a special CD-ROM disk drive to your computer. Data is etched onto the surface of a CD in the form of microscopic pits. A laser in the CD-ROM disk drive "reads" the pattern of pits, translates it into binary code, and sends the data to the computer.

You also need retrieval software that tells the computer how to find specific information on the CD and how to display it on the computer screen.

CD-ROM's biggest advantage is its storage capacity. One compact disk just 4.72 inches in diameter can store up to 700MB of data. For example, the entire text of *The New Grolier Electronic Encyclopedia* — a 20-volume set in standard print form — is available on a single CD-ROM. And it takes up only about one-fifth of the disk! The rest of the space is used for illustrations from the encyclopedia.

CD-ROM is especially useful for storing multimedia programs, reference information, catalogs, graphic images, legal precedents, and medical data. One company has stored a list of 370,000 poisons and their antidotes on a CD that is being used by hospitals. When the name of a poison is typed into the computer, the correct antidote appears on the screen. The system will even calculate the correct dosage, based on the weight of the victim.

Chapter Three

COMPUTER SOFTWARE

Computers do something you probably wish people did: they do exactly what you tell them to do. They follow instructions. In fact, the *only* thing they do is follow instructions. Without instructions, they just sit there, as useless as that proverbial bump on a log.

A list of instructions that tells a computer what to do is called a program, or software. A program can be as short as PRINT "HELLO." Or it can contain tens of thousands of instructions.

Some people enjoy designing and writing their own software. This requires a talent for thinking logically, plus a knowledge of computer programming, including the ability to "speak" at least one computer language (see box). It also requires time and patience. A mistyped word, the wrong punctuation mark, or an error in logic will prevent the program from running, or cause it to behave in unexpected ways. Before a program is usable, all the errors must be removed.

The vast majority of computer users buy off-the-shelf software, or acquire free public-domain software (see Chapter Five). There are many thousands of packages from which to choose. In the word-processing arena alone, there are hundreds of competing titles; many are designed to meet the needs of specific audiences — young children, families, small businesses, large corporations, and so on.

Each of the applications discussed in this chapter can be purchased individually. Many also are available in integrated packages, which contain somewhat-abbreviated versions of a cluster of applications. For example, the popular *Microsoft Works* includes word processing, spreadsheet, database, and communications applications.

COMPUTER LANGUAGES

Want to tell a computer to add 5 plus 7? If you gave instructions in machine language — the binary code understood by the computer — it would look like this:

```
001000000101100011111100000110001111100010101001000001
010110100100000111100011010010011000000111101101000100
101001001010010010100100101000101001000011110110100011
011000000100000111011011111110110101101001001110000001
100101001000011110001100001101001101100000010000001110
11011111110 100100000110100000000001100000000
```

It's not surprising that programmers — people who write computer software — do not work in machine language! Instead, they usually write in a *high-level language*. Then they use a special program to translate their instructions into machine language instructions.

There are many high-level languages, each with its own vocabulary, grammar, and syntax. In addition, most languages come in several versions, each designed for certain purposes or computers. Widely used high-level languages include ADA, ALGOL, BASIC, C, COBOL, FORTH, FORTRAN, LISP, LOGO, Pascal, PROLOG, and SmallTalk.

WORD PROCESSING

The most popular computer application is word processing — using the computer to write text. Anyone who has ever written a report of any sort can appreciate word processing's benefits.

When you write a report by hand or with a typewriter, you soon have a mess: crossed-out lines, sentences in the margins that must to be inserted, arrows indicating where paragraphs need to be moved, and so on. Eventually you finish, producing a clean manuscript. Then you discover a mistyped word. Or you realize you should have added another sentence to the second paragraph. You face the question: is it worth retyping the report to make this change?

With word processing, writing, rewriting, and printing are a snap. You can quickly erase sentences, correct typographical errors, move paragraphs around, and add information. And you do it all without erasers, scissors, glue sticks, or swear words.

Basically, word processing allows you to do two things:

- Write a document, known as editing
- Prepare the document for printing, known as formatting.

Editing Options

Anything you write with a word processor is called a document. You type in text just as you would on a typewriter. When you begin, the display screen (your "sheet of paper") is blank except for a small, movable spot of light called the cursor. The cursor indicates where the first character you type will appear. As you type, the cursor moves. You also can move the cursor by using the arrow keys on the keyboard.

The word processing program contains many editing options. Let's say you're writing a letter. You want to move a paragraph from the beginning of the letter to another location in the letter. You begin by marking the paragraph. In one word processing program, this is done by moving the cursor to the beginning of the first line of the paragraph and then pressing the function key F6. Next, you move the cursor to the end of the paragraph and press F6 again.

These two steps mark the block of text to be moved and highlight it, so that you can confirm you marked the correct text. Now move the cursor to the place where you want to insert the paragraph. Press F6. OK? Then press F5 and the move is complete. But if you change your mind and want to move the paragraph elsewhere, continue on with the cursor to the new location and press F6 again. You can do this as many times as you want before pressing F5 to finalize the command.

Describing the process takes MUCH longer than actually doing it! Editing options are performed very speedily — much, much faster than a beginning user can imagine.

Editing options available on most programs include:

Block move   Define a block of text and then move it to another location, either within the same document or to another document.

Delete   Erase text. Using different commands, you can delete a letter, a word, a line, or a large block of text.

File insertion   Insert, or merge, a file stored on a disk into the file you currently are editing.

Global search and replace   Use of a single command to locate all occurrences of a word or phrase in a document. You then have the option of changing these on an individual basis or using a command to do a global replace — that is, replace the word or phrase everywhere that it occurs (i.e., globally) with a different word or phrase.

Insert and **typeover**   Add new text at any point within a document. In insert mode, already entered text is pushed ahead as you type in new text. In typeover mode, new text replaces previously entered text.

Scroll   Move text or other material either horizontally (right/left) or vertically (up/down) on the display screen. This allows you to read through a document that is too long or too wide to fit on the screen.

Undelete   Retrieve text deleted by a previous delete command. (The program holds deleted text in a special memory area until the next time you delete text from the document.)

Word count   Count the number of words in a document or in part of a document.

Word wrap   The automatic movement of a word too long to fit on a line to the next line. This feature is comparable to pressing the carriage return on a typewriter, except that word wrap is automatic.

DEFAULT COMMANDS

Computers have predefined responses to certain commands. They choose this response unless you specify otherwise. For example, if your system has two or more disk drives, one of them will be the default drive. The computer goes there to look for a program you want to load — unless you tell it to look at the disk in another drive.

Many programs also have default settings. For example, in a word processing program a document may automatically be printed 50 lines to a page, with 10 characters per inch, unless you give the program different instructions.

Default settings can be changed. If you almost always want to print 55 lines per page, you should change the default setting in your word processing program from 50 to 55, following directions in the program manual. Then you won't have to give a page length command every time you want to print a document at 55 lines per page.

Formatting Options

Using various commands in the word processing program, you can indicate how you want the printed document to look. This is called formatting. Some programs let you see on the display screen exactly how the formatted document will look when it's printed; this is on-screen formatting. Other programs store the formatting instructions but you don't see the results until the document is printed; this is off-screen formatting.

Common formatting options include:

Automatic hyphenation   Insert a hyphen in the word at the end of a line, thereby making the line break properly at the right margin.

Automatic pagination   Print sequential page numbers on a document.

Centering   Position titles, lines of poetry, or other text in the middle of a line.

Headers and footers   Print a line of text, such as a chapter title, at the top (header) or bottom (footer) of a page. You can specify on which pages these should appear (all pages, right-hand pages only, etc.).

Justification   Align text along a margin; the margin is straight, as opposed to ragged. Text typically is justified along the left-hand margin, and is said to be flush left. Justification along the right-hand margin as well (flush right) requires the program to add extra spacing after punctuation marks and between words to fill out the line.

Line spacing   Print text "solid" or add one or more lines of space between every two lines of text. Adding one line of space is called double-spacing; adding two lines of space is called triple-spacing.

Margin settings   Decide how large to make the margins along the top, sides, and bottom of the page.

Page display   View on the display screen where text will "break" when it is printed. This helps you to avoid bad page breaks. For example, if only one line of a letter is left to be printed on a second page, you can edit the text so that it fits on a single sheet.

Page length   Indicate the maximum number of lines to be printed on a page.

Text enhancement   Use boldface, underlining, italics, compressed type, subscripts (as in H_2O), superscripts (as in 4^{10}), and other special effects.

Accessory Programs

Many word processing programs include two very useful accessory programs:

Spell checker   This program checks the spelling of words in your documents. Each word in a document is compared to words in a built-in dictionary. Words not found in the dictionary are highlighted and you are asked to verify that they are correct. You can customize the dictionary, adding technical terms, abbreviations, and other terms that you use frequently.

Watch! A spell checker only checks that words are spelled correctly; it cannot determine if the words are used correctly. For example, a spell checker would not find anything wrong with this sentence: We tells there mutter wear two by meet.

Electronic thesaurus   This program provides synonyms for tens of thousands of words. It's great for those times when you can't think of the best word to use, as well as times when you find yourself using the same word over and over again.

DATABASE MANAGEMENT SYSTEMS

A metal file cabinet holds dozens of files. Two cabinets hold even more files — and take up even more space. Instead of filling rooms with cabinets, you can use a database management system (DBMS) and put all the information on disks; a few disks have a greater capacity than several drawers in a file cabinet! In addition to saving space, you gain these benefits:

- Data can be accessed, sorted, cross-referenced, and analyzed instantly.
- Data can be collated into a report, chart, or other document, which can then be printed.
- Data can easily be shared among computer users, improving efficiency and cutting down on duplication of data otherwise held in separate places.

The purpose of a DBMS is to organize collections of data. Any type of data can be made easier to maintain and much more accessible: membership files, checking accounts, restaurant reservations, mailing lists, employee records, batting records of current and past National League players, and so on. A general application DBMS can handle all of these. In addition, there are customized programs for specific needs or industries.

You'll follow three steps when you use a DBMS:

- Create a format for the database
- Enter data using the format
- Retrieve information from the database.

Creating a Database

The first and most important step in setting up a database is creating the format for the records you'll store in that database. A record must have a logical, consistent structure. And all the records in a database must have the exact same structure. This structure has three parts:

- Field: An item of information, such as a person's name.
- Record: A collection of related fields, such as the person's name, street address, town, state, zip code, telephone number, and fax number.
- File: A collection of related records, such as a telephone directory.

Use index cards to create and experiment with different structures. Try to imagine all the ways in which you might want to access the data at some future time. Might you wish to send a mailing to all customers who own late-model Toyotas? Then you need fields named CAR BRAND and MODEL YEAR. To people earning at least $50,000 a year? Add a field named INCOME. Only to women? Add a field named SEX.

DATABASE RECORDS

```
                                                              Field
   FILE: Company Telephone Extensions                         names

   Last name        First name      Phone         Dept
  ┌Hacker          Jeff            555-3784       Systems
  ┌Jackson         Judy            555-3751       Marketing
  ┌Prescott        Wendy           555-3732       Accounting
  ┌Rodriguez       Carlos          555-3719       Editorial

 └─ Rows                           Fields
```

As you tell the DBMS the structure for the records, you also indicate the maximum number of spaces needed to accommodate the information in each field. Give yourself enough room. If you leave eight spaces for surnames, a record for someone named Brackenbill will be abbreviated to Brackenb.

You also tell the program what kind of data will be allowed in each field. An alphanumeric field contains letters, numbers, and special characters — basically, anything you can type on the computer keyboard. A numeric field contains only numbers. A currency field contains dollar values. This makes data entry more efficient and less prone to errors. For example, the program won't accept a city name in the telephone number field; if you enter 45983.488 into a currency field, the program automatically changes it to $45,983.49.

Now you're ready to enter data into the system. Most DBMS used fixed formats. For each record, you bring up a blank form onto the display screen. Then you fill in the form, much like you'd fill in a paper form. Here's a filled-in record in a person's database of video tapes he owns:

TITLE: Fine Romance, A
YEAR: 1992
DIRECTOR: Saks, Gene
WRITER: Harwood, Ronald
MALE LEAD: Mastroianni, Marcello
FEMALE LEAD: Andrews, Julie

If needed, the record can be easily deleted or corrected. But adding a field would necessitate going back and adding it to every single record in the database.

Using a Database

Once all the records have been entered, you can put the program to work for you. Most DBMS have a feature called a report generator, which allows you to indicate how the program should print or display data. Possibilities are almost endless!

The owner of the video-tape database might ask for a list of all his tapes directed by Gene Saks, or all those starring both

Andrews and Mastroianni. But he couldn't ask for a list of films he could view in less than 90 minutes because such a field is not part of the records.

A computer retailer might ask for a printout of customers who own Atari computers. A school administrator might request a list of employees and their salaries, with the salaries subtotaled by school or job classification. A florist may request a list of customers who spend at least $200 a year and have birthdays in June.

Program Features

Key features of database programs include:

Query   List data from all the records, such as the titles of all films released in 1992.

Search   Find a specific field, such as the name of the male lead in *A Fine Romance*.

Wild cards   Search for records when you don't remember the exact spelling. To search for Mastroianni, you might use Mas*, with the asterisk representing any number of characters in that position. Of course, the program will display all surnames in the database that begin with Mas. However, you could narrow the search to male leads whose surnames begin with these letters.

Sort   List records alphabetically or numerically by a selected field. You could sort the video tape collection by title or by year of release.

Data Import   Enter information from another application, such as a spreadsheet where you listed the costs of all the video tapes you've purchased. This saves you from having to type in the data again.

Merge   Combine database information with form letters. Using files from your mailing list database, you could send an invitation to all your friends inviting them to a showing of *A Fine Romance*.

Security Databases often contain an organization's most valuable information, which makes security a critical issue. Most commonly, security features take the form of secret passwords or codes that limit access to all or part of a database. For example, an employer might allow secretaries to access employee name and telephone-extension fields but not salary and age fields.

ELECTRONIC SPREADSHEETS

Combine a pencil, an eraser, paper, and a calculator into one package and what do you get? An electronic spreadsheet! These programs save hours and even days of time, and take much of the agony out of such tasks as preparing budgets, tracking expenses, determining the effects of price changes on future earnings, and computing loan payments.

Spreadsheets are used mainly for financial calculations. But they also can be used in other situations that involve large numbers of figures. Teachers use them to calculate students' grades and uncover student achievement patterns. Meteorologists use them to track precipitation. Medical researchers use them to organize experimental data.

Creating a Spreadsheet

A spreadsheet consists of a grid of boxes, or cells. Each horizontal group of cells is called a row. A vertical stack of cells is called a column. Rows are identified by numbers running down the left-hand side of the spreadsheet, beginning with the number 1. Columns are identified by letters running across the top, beginning with the letter A (A through Z for the first 26 columns, AA through ZZ for the next 26, etc.).

Some programs allow you to create spreadsheets with hundreds of columns and thousands of rows. Only a small section of a large spreadsheet can fit onto a display screen. To view another section, you scroll the spreadsheet (use arrow keys or a mouse to move it up, down, right, or left on the screen).

At first, all the cells in a spreadsheet are empty. The spreadsheet looks like this:

	A	B	C	D	E
1					
2					
3					
4					
5					

Each cell is identified by an address, which consists of its column letter followed by its row number. The cell in the upper left-hand corner is A1. To its right is B1. Under A1 is A2.

What goes into a cell? One of three things:

- A label, such as a budget category, type of exercise, or name of player
- A number that expresses a quantity, such as a dollar amount, number of calories burned, or golf score
- A formula that calculates the value of the cell.

Before you begin to enter data into a spreadsheet, take time to decide the scope of the document, the components it must contain, where the various components should be placed, and what equations will produce the results you want.

Let's say you want to compile office expenses. Here's the sample spreadsheet after some labels, numbers, and formulas have been entered:

	A	B	C	D	E
1		January	February	March	Quarter
2	Supplies	13.50	8.46	19.30	41.26
3	Telephone	88.27	75.00		
4	Electric	191.75	160.27		
5	Insurance	227.98	227.98		
6	TOTAL	521.50			

All the cells in row one and column A contain labels. Formulas were placed in cells E2 and B6. Cell E2 has been defined as equalling B2+C2+D2. If you change the value of one of these three cells, the program recalculates the value of E2. For example, if you change B2 to 14.50, E2 immediately changes to 42.26. At the same time, B6 changes to 522.50 because it has been defined as B2+B3+B4+B5.

Numbers and formulas have not yet been placed in some of the cells in our spreadsheet. Cell E3 needs to be defined as B3+C3+D3. As soon as this is done, 163.27 will appear in that cell, even though no value has yet been given for D3.

This example demonstrates the power of electronic spreadsheets. Make one change and all the other figures affected by that change are recalcuated automatically!

What-If Analysis

Because spreadsheet programs can perform complex calculations amazingly quickly, many people use them to make projections or forecasts. This is called what-if analysis. For example, you might use a spreadsheet to determine:

- WHAT would happen to your investment income IF interest rates rose one percent?
- WHAT would happen to company profits IF each employee were given a bonus equal to one week's paycheck?
- WHAT changes would you have to make in your budget IF your medical insurance payments jumped $58 a month?
- HOW many additional T-shirts would you have to sell to keep earnings steady IF you lowered the price of T-shirts by $10 a dozen — or by $20 a dozen or $30 a dozen?

In other words, once the spreadsheet is set up with labels and formulas, you can plug in any numbers you want, see what happens, then erase the numbers and test other data.

Program Features

Common features of spreadsheet programs include:

Functions Predefined formulas that you can insert into your spreadsheets; for example, formulas that calculate the amount of depreciation in a specific period, the future value of an annuity, and the number of days between two dates.

Sorting Change the way that data are organized; for example, a list of employees or stocks can be sorted so that the names are in alphabetical order.

Consolidation Load (consolidate) data from several spreadsheets into a single spreadsheet.

Charting Display and print out spreadsheet data in chart form (bar charts, pie charts, etc).

Data import and export Move data files to and from other spreadsheet programs, database programs, etc.

Printing features Print spreadsheets sideways or compress spreadsheets in order to fit more columns onto one page.

IT'S A NO-NO!

Computer piracy — copying software without permission of the copyright holder — is illegal. You're violating the U.S. Copyright Law if you make a copy of your favorite game for a buddy, or if you buy a spreadsheet program and make copies for other employees in your company.

The only exception is a purchaser's right to make a backup copy of a program. The purchaser can then work with the backup copy and keep the original copy in a safe place, to be used when and if the backup copy is damaged. Neither copy may legally be used by anyone else.

The Software Publishers Association, the principal trade group of the pc software industry, has filed dozens of lawsuits citing copyright infringement. In most cases, settlements are reached, with cash payments earmarked for use in fighting similar cases. Some of those settlements have been mighty big!

GRAPHICS PROGRAMS

Graphics software lets you create your own pictures. These programs range from fun programs for young children to easy-to-master business-oriented programs to highly sophisticated programs for professionals in various industries.

Applications are equally varied: you can create banners, greeting cards, cartoons for newsletters, stationery letterheads, charts and maps, copies of famous drawings, highly detailed engineering schematics . . . and doodles. The illustrations in this book were created with graphics software.

There are two distinct types of computer images:

Bit-mapped image Saved ("mapped") in computer memory as a pattern of bits; each pixel on the display screen is represented by its own bit(s). Examples include photographic images and "freehand" drawings.

Object-oriented image Saved in computer memory as mathematical formulas that describe the object's shape, the start and end point of each line, the curve of arcs, etc. Examples include building plans, product designs, and technical illustrations.

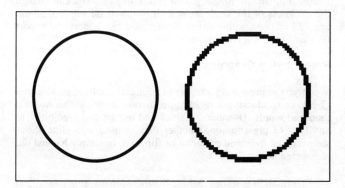

Object-oriented circle   Bit-mapped circle

Paint Programs

Paint programs are used to create bit-mapped images. You use your mouse to click onto a paintbrush, make a drawing, then dip into paint cans and fill in areas with color. You can erase and redraw, zoom in to get a close-up look at a section, zoom back to view the entire drawing, and so on. Other tools at your disposal include:

- Draw: creates predesigned shapes such as circles, ovals, and rectangles
- Lasso: draws a line around an object so that you can cut, copy, move, erase, or make other changes to it
- Spray paint: puts color or patterns on an object; you can adjust the spray to create shading
- Text: lets you add titles, labels, and other words
- Import: allows you to load in graphics from other programs
- Export: allows you to insert your drawing into another program.

Draw Programs

Draw programs create object-oriented images. There are tools to draw lines, rectangles, circles, and ovals. Other tools let you manipulate and change the objects you draw. You can move, copy, rotate, flip, stretch, magnify, and shrink objects. You can change the thickness of lines, fill areas with color, create subtle shading, and add text. As with paint programs, you can import and export files and there's a zoom feature.

Presentation Graphics

When you're presenting a report to your class, selling an idea to a client, or conducting a meeting, a picture truly can be worth a thousand words. Dynamic graphics add impact and credibility to any type of presentation, whether they're used as a slide show, shown on an overhead projector or flipchart, or simply handed out to your audience.

Presentation graphics include diagrams, maps, title pages, and all sorts of charts. They are designed to be succinct and easy to

TYPES OF CHARTS

Bar chart Uses either horizontal or vertical rectangles called bars; effective for comparing numerical data, such as annual ice cream consumption in various countries or number of AIDS deaths over the past ten years.

Bullet chart Lists several items, each preceded by a small circle, or bullet; good for presenting groups of things, such as the five main features of a product.

Gantt chart Uses horizontal bar segments to indicate time periods; used to illustrate how long various components of a project will take and the scheduling relationships among the components.

High-low chart Uses vertical lines to represent the range between the highest and lowest values within a category; commonly used to track stock market prices.

Line chart Dots representing numerical data are connected by lines; good for showing trends and comparing chronological data, such as sales volume over the past five years.

Pie chart Divides a circle ("pie") into segments to show relative magnitudes of the various parts; useful for comparing parts of a whole, such as budget categories. An exploding pie chart separates out one wedge of the pie for emphasis.

Table chart Arranges data in rows and columns; effective for presenting precise textual information, such as names of countries, their capitals, and their heads of state.

read, so that viewers can absorb the message quickly, without losing track of what you, the speaker, are saying.

Presentation graphics software — plus a little imagination — enables you to make charts far classier than anything you might do by hand. Need a chart showing how many bushels of apples were produced in your state over the past five years? You could make a

bar chart with five vertical columns, with each column representing a year. Or, using clip art, you could replace those ordinary
columns with columns of shiny red apples.

Presentation graphics tools are part of many larger graphics
packages. They also are sold as separate packages that have the
ability to work with popular applications programs. For instance,
you can use data from a spreadsheet or database to create a chart.
Or you can put a visual created with the presentation graphics program into a newsletter you're creating with your desktop publishing program.

Computer-Assisted Design (CAD)

Design is a critical but time-consuming step in the creation of any
object, whether it's a house, ship engine, bottle, or sneaker.
Computer-assisted design (CAD) software saves time and
improves the precision and accuracy of drawings, resulting in
fewer problems later in the production cycle. It allows designers to
easily make changes and to quickly produce multiple copies of
similar drawings.

CAD programs are draw programs. They are used to produce
three-dimensional images composed of circles, arcs, and straight
lines. Many packages have a symbols library filled with frequently used drawings. For example, CAD software for electronic engineers has a library of transistors, capacitors, and other parts that
the engineers can insert into their drawings of electric circuits.
CAD software for interior decorators includes drawings of tables,
chairs, and bathtubs.

An image can be rotated and viewed from different angles. It
can be expanded or shrunk. Some CAD programs have a zoom
feature that enables the user to magnify, or zoom in on, parts of
the design. For example, an architect can show a client the exteri-
or of a building, then zoom in onto the design of a particular window or even into each room in the building.

The program stores not only the design but also information
about the design. Data on a telephone model includes colors,
dimensions, materials used for each part, even how the telephone
should be constructed.

CLIP ART

You don't have to be an artist to dress up presentations, newsletters, brochures, and other material with graphic images. Commercial collections of *clip art* offer thousands of images stored on disks and ready to be electronically "clipped out" and "pasted into" documents.

Clip art includes borders, cartoon characters, symbols, flags, maps, arrows, animals, flowers, sporting equipment, pointing hands, musical notes, airplanes, holiday objects — almost everything imaginable.

Many graphics, presentation, and other software packages include libraries of clip art. You can also buy separate collections, then "import" the desired graphics into your applications. (Just make sure that the clip-art packages are compatible with your application software!)

DESKTOP PUBLISHING

Thanks to desktop publishing programs, anyone can become a publisher. This software has transformed the field of publishing, opening it up to people who could never before afford to publish. It's enabled companies to reap enormous savings by producing brochures, forms, and other documents in-house instead of farming the work out to typesetting firms and graphics houses. And it's improved the appearance of everything from club newsletters and office memos to glossy advertisements and product manuals.

Major desktop publishing programs let you import data from other application programs, including word processing, database, spreadsheet, and graphics programs. You also can use a scanner to convert photographs, drawings, and printed text into computer files, which can then be used by your desktop publishing program.

You can arrange the material on each page in any way you want. Experiment with:

- Multiple columns of text
- Wrapping text around graphics
- Different typefaces (but make sure that your printer can print them)
- Titles of various sizes
- Shrinking, magnifying, and cropping graphics.

When everything is arranged the way you want it, the results will look best if they're printed out on a laser printer.

Program Features

In addition to commands that allow you to do the things listed above, many desktop publishing programs include such features as:

Automatic numbering   Automatically numbers chapters, pages, tables, and other elements.

Drawing tools   Let you create lines, squares, circles, and rectangles; for example, you might want to put some text in a box, or draw a circle around a piece of cartoon art.

Hyphenation   Some programs handle this automatically; others require you to do the chore manually.

Kerning   Lets you adjust the spacing between letters, to make words look more attractive; generally used for large type, such as that used in headlines.

WYSIWIG   Stands for "what you see is what you get", means you work on the screen with an exact representation of the final printed document.

EDUCATION AND TRAINING

Using computers to learn information and skills offers certain advantages over traditional methods. Students can work at their own pace. They are encouraged to experiment — no one will laugh at them or reprimand them for mistakes. They are in control, and have their "teacher's" undivided attention. Furthermore, this teacher has infinite patience; it will repeat instructions or information over and over again if necessary.

There are three major types of educational software:

Tutorials   These programs use step-by-step instructions to teach facts, skills, and concepts. Tutorials teach people how to operate a piece of equipment, use punctuation, read music, play the guitar, and program computers.

Tutorials are rather like textbooks, except that they are interactive. Information is presented in small units, each followed by questions that test the user's comprehension. If incorrect answers are given, the program reviews the material, perhaps presenting it in a different way.

Drill and practice   These programs are used to reinforce skills in subjects such as arithmetic, spelling, speed reading, foreign languages, and typing. The best examples are highly interactive. They keep track of a user's mistakes, then use this information to determine the level of difficulty and kinds of questions to ask. Many drill programs have color, sound, and graphics, and take the form of games; for example, a child may have to solve addition problems to outsmart roaring dragons.

Simulations   These programs imitate real events. How do you pilot a plane? What decisions need to be made to improve your candidate's chances of election? What challenges would you face as head of a Fortune 500 company, and how would you handle those challenges? What happens during a volcanic eruption?

At the same time that they teach or reinforce facts and concepts, simulations help users appreciate the multiple cause-and-effect relationships inherent in most situations. If you don't navigate a tanker properly, you run around and spill oil. If a snowstorm eats up a larger-than-planned part of the city budget, you have to make cuts elsewhere.

GENERAL BUSINESS PROGRAMS

The applications discussed so far in this chapter are commonly used by people of all ages, for many different purposes. In addition, there's a cornucopia of software designed to help people run their businesses. For example:

- If you're thinking of launching a new product or business, there are programs designed to help you develop and implement a business plan.
- If you don't have an employee manual, there are programs that contain dozens of company policy statements, which you can use verbatim or edit to meet your specific needs.
- If composing letters, contracts, and other documents is a chore you hate, there are software collections of letters of agreement, contracts, order forms, request forms, termination notices, etc.
- If you do lots of mailings, there are programs that print labels and envelopes, have templates for U.S. Postal Service airbills, perform ZIP-Code sorts, etc.

Accounting Software

To function smoothly, every business must keep track of money: what it receives, what it spends, what it is owed, and so on. If these tasks are not handled on a frequent basis, the business soon ends up with stacks of unpaid invoices, late billings, and other costly problems. Accounting packages include the following tools:

- General ledger: records financial transactions, tracks assets and liabilities, and generates balance sheets and income statements.
- Accounts receivable: tracks moneys owed by customers or clients.
- Invoicing: prepares invoices.
- Accounts payable: tracks invoices received from vendors and determines when they should be paid, based on cash-flow analysis; may include a check-writing program.
- Payroll: calculates each employee's taxes and other deductions, prints a check for the employee's net pay, prepares end-of-the-year government payroll filings.

EXAMPLES OF SPECIALIZED BUSINESS SOFTWARE

Occupation	Software
Auto mechanic	vibration diagnostics
Banker	loan amortization
Building contractor	job costing
Courtroom stenographer	transcription
Farmer	herd breeding and management
Forest firefighter	wind + weather analysis
Librarian	cataloging
Market researcher	public opinion analysis
Minister	church membership tracking
Petroleum scientist	seismic data analysis
Physician	practice billing
Realtor	property management
Shipper	package labeling
Telemarketer	list management
Trade show producer	show registration
Trucker	fleet maintenance
Viniculturist	wine inventory

Project Management Software

Project management software helps managers plan and keep track of the tasks, resources, time schedules, and costs of a project. Whether overseeing production of a movie or construction of a skyscraper, a manager can break down the undertaking into a series of smaller activities, chart time and sequence requirements of these activities, identify potential scheduling problems, define staff requirements, generate budgets and reports, compare actual versus planned schedules, and so on.

Like spreadsheets, this software is useful for investigating "what-if" situations: What happens to the production schedule for a book if the manuscript arrives a week late? What happens to the budget if we add more color photographs?

Statistical Packages

Statistical analysis software are powerful tools that use a variety of calculations to analyze large sets of data. They determine if the data are statistically meaningful, compute probabilities, identify patterns, and present results in formats that are relevant and understandable to the intended audience. Many statistical packages have built-in graphics so that users can use data to create charts or maps.

Decision Support Tools

Managers must constantly make decisions based on a variety of factors: Considering your limited budget, which projects should you undertake? Should money be put into print ads or trade shows? Which sales incentive plan should you choose?

Decision support programs help you define the important criteria involved in making a particular decision. You assign a numerical value, or weight, to each criterion. Then you score each of your options to see which ranks highest.

Let's say you're considering applicants for a job. Based on your knowledge and experience, you decide that 40 percent of the weight should be given to experience directly related to the job, 20 percent to technical knowledge, 20 percent to references, 10 percent to salary demands, and 10 percent to education. You rate the candidates in a consistent manner, based on something more concrete than "gut feelings."

SELF-IMPROVEMENT AND ENTERTAINMENT

There are computer programs for almost any personal interest or activity. This small sampling gives you a sense of the scope of what's available:

Garden planners Help you choose plants best suited for your geographical area, lay out your garden, and determine optimal planting and harvesting dates.

Geneology programs Help you organize information about your ancestors and create family trees.

Home inventory programs   For people who have everything, or at least want to protect everything they have against financial loss in case of fire, theft, or natural disaster.

Legal forms portfolios   Provide forms for wills, power of attorney, living trusts, and other legal documents, which can be edited to meet your particular needs.

Résumé kits   Help you prepare professional résumés, cover letters, interview thank-you letters, and other documents you may need as you try to land that perfect job.

Wedding planners   Help you prepare guest lists, schedule events, choose honeymoon destinations, and keep track of estimated and actual expenses.

Health and Fitness

Medical programs   Provide information on diseases, injuries, medical tests, immunizations, nutrition, dieting, and fitness, and make diagnoses based on an analysis of your symptoms.

Cookbook programs   Contain recipes, often with nutritional information and weight-loss plans.

Exercise programs   Offer a variety of basic routines or a customized routine that provides extra toning in specific body areas.

Biofeedback programs   Designed to teach you how to handle stress, how to relax, even how to control blood pressure and heart rate.

Money Matters

Money managers   Organize your bills, write checks, reconcile accounts, track insurance policies, set up stock and bond portfolios, forecast cash flow, and calculate your net worth.

Credit-management programs   Keep track of your lines of credit and help you check for and correct inaccuracies in your credit report.

Tax programs Guide you through tax preparation, from compiling the necessary data to printing out tax forms for federal and state income taxes.

Retirement programs Guide you through the steps involved in setting up a financial retirement plan.

Game Software

Journey through caverns of an underground empire. Use your helicopters to rescue kidnapped U.N. delegates. Maneuver a frisky, dot-gobbling character around a maze. Lead a battalion of Civil War soldiers. Defend your pasture against a giant centipede. Coach the football team of your dreams. Venture into remote jungles. Knock off aliens. Dodge enemy UFOs.

Many people won't admit it, but playing games is a great reason for having a computer. In fact, the popularity of computer games in the 1970s was a major stimulus for the development of inexpensive pc's — people were buying the machines to play *Breakout* and *Space Invaders* years before they thought of using those computers for business purposes!

Well-designed computer games provide hour after hour of enjoyment. They remain challenging because they provide multiple levels of difficulty — as you master play at one level you can test your skills at a more advanced level of play. Many give you the option of playing against the computer or with a friend. Super graphics, sound effects, and even digitized speech add to the excitement.

There's something for everyone. Major categories include:

Arcade games Games that let you shoot at aliens or some other targets and try to pile up ever-higher scores. Good eye-hand coordination and quick reflexes are important.

Fantasy role-playing games Text-based stories in which you constantly have to make decisions: Which path should I follow? Are these people to be trusted? What's the meaning of this riddle? Is this water safe to drink?

Games of chance and skill   Electronic versions of card games such as bridge and poker, board games such as *Monopoly* and *Scrabble*, and tv shows such as *Jeopardy!* and *Wheel of Fortune*.

Simulations   Games that use graphics and sound effects to imitate real-life situations, giving you the chance to live vicariously as you pilot a jet fighter, drive a Formula One car, play pool with Minnesota Fats, invest your savings on the stock market, or guide a wagon train along the Oregon Trail during the 1840s.

UTILITY PROGRAMS

After you've used your computer system for a while, you'll wish there were a way to use simpler commands, squeeze more data onto your hard disk, or recover a data file you mistakenly erased. Fortunately, many of these wishes are easily granted. Computer programmers have created hundreds of small, inexpensive programs called utilities. Utilities are designed to perform certain housekeeping and maintenance tasks. They improve your efficiency and the efficiency of your computer system, protect the system against various disasters, and enable you to say goodbye to dull and annoying chores.

Most utilities are memory-resident programs. That is, they remain in the computer's memory at all times. You can access them instantly, even when you're in the middle of an application. Perhaps you're writing a report and need to add up a column of numbers. Instead of using a calculator on your desk, you press one or two keys on your keyboard to display a calculator on the monitor. Do the calculations, then press another key to return to your report.

Many utilities are packaged with operating systems and application programs. For example, utilities included with MS-DOS can display a list of files stored on a disk, copy files from one disk to another, and erase unwanted files on a disk. Spell checkers and thesauruses included in word processing packages also can be thought of as utilities.

Numerous additional utilities are sold separately. Some packages include a broad range of features, others focus on a specific function. Particularly useful utilities include:

File recovery programs   These utilities can recover files that you mistakenly erased from a floppy or hard disk. Some can also recover files from disks that have been damaged.

Compressors   At first, you may think that your 30MB or 60MB hard disk has more space than you'll ever need. But newer application programs, especially those for business, require lots of storage space. Before long, you're likely to find yourself running out of room. Compressors are utilities that compress data, giving you extra space so that you can fit more files onto a hard or floppy disk.

Macro makers   Performing the same sequence of commands over and over is time-consuming. Do you telephone your mother every day? Each time, you can dial all the digits in her telephone number. But if your phone lets you record frequently called numbers, all you have to do is press a certain key combination and the phone dials the number for you.

DESKTOP ORGANIZERS

- Are you fed up having to deal with — and trying to find amid the clutter in your office — calendars, appointment books, to-do lists, calculators, and other items that are supposed to make your life easier?
- Is "getting organized" your #1 New Year's resolution?

Solve such problems with a desktop organizer, or desk manager. This is a memory-resident utility that contains a variety of tools, such as an appointment calendar, monthly calendar, address book, notebook, calculator, alarm clock, and phone dialer.

Here's how a desktop organizer works: Say you're working on a spreadsheet or other application and you want to look up an address. You can temporarily exit the application by pressing a few keys. Get the address, perhaps make a note on your appointment calendar, then return to where you left off in the application.

A macro maker works in much the same way. It lets you assign a sequence of commands to one or two keys that you aren't using for another purpose. The macros you create in this manner are stored in the program for future use.

Macro makers are built into newer versions of MS-DOS and *Windows*, and into many application programs. For example, you may write many letters to customers, thanking them for their orders. You use the same paragraph in all the letters. You can save the paragraph on a disk and assign a macro to it, perhaps a combination of the CONTROL and P keys. Then, whenever you reach the point in a letter where you want to insert the paragraph, all you have to do is press Ctl-P. (If you purchase a separate macro maker, be sure it's compatible with the software you already own.)

Printer utilities These programs enhance printer operations by allowing you to schedule print times, drive multiple printers simultaneously, print spreadsheets sideways, etc.

Screen savers If an image is left on the monitor screen for too long, the image may burn into the screen — and you'll see it forever after. One way to avoid this problem is to dim or turn off the monitor when you're not using it. Another solution is to install a screen saver program. When you do not use the keyboard or other input device for several minutes, the screen saver either blanks the screen or displays ever-changing images such as swimming fish, floating flowers, or whirling kaleidoscopes. As soon as you touch the input device, your original image is restored.

Anti-virus programs These utilities protect computers and computer networks against harmful programs called viruses (see Chapter Six).

MULTIMEDIA

As you listen to a high-quality CD recording of Beethoven's Ninth Symphony as played by the Vienna Philaharmonic, a running commentary about this masterpiece is displayed on your computer screen. If you wish, you can follow Beethoven's score. Curious about a recurring melody? Stop the music. Press a key and one of the world's leading experts on Beethoven discusses the defiance theme. Go back and listen again to the theme. Jump to other places in the symphony where the theme recurs. At the conclusion of the music, read about the audience's reaction at the Viennese premiere of the symphony on May 7, 1824.

Multimedia Beethoven: The Ninth Symphony demonstrates the rich possibilities of multimedia, a technology that brings together text, graphics, animated sequences, video, music and voice. Multimedia is in its infancy but growing rapidly. It is transforming and enriching the meaning of the term *computer software*, and extending the use of computers into new areas. With the proper hardware and software, you can:

- Add your voice to Monday morning messages delivered to your employees via E-mail, or to a spreadsheet report to document your assumptions and explain how you arrived at your conclusions.
- Create animated repair manuals for equipment, complete with step-by-step video instructions and 3-D images that can be viewed from any angle.
- Turn those video tapes you shot on your last vacation into a film complete with music, animated title screens, voice-overs, and computer-generated maps.

Creating and viewing multimedia   Multimedia productions require the following equipment:

- A pc with a high-speed microprocessor, a graphics card capable of displaying high-quality images, an audio subsystem, and a mouse
- A high-capacity hard disk drive
- A CD-ROM drive.

Depending on the features you wish to incorporate in a multimedia production, you may also want such equipment as a microphone to input voice, a musical keyboard, and a mixer to combine sounds. Creating multimedia also requires special software known as authoring software. This software takes the disparate elements and converts them into one seamless presentation. It handles such tasks as design, data management, editing (croping video clips, making CAD drawings, etc.), synchronization, and testing of the finished presentation.

Chapter Four

COMPUTER COMMUNICATIONS

When you bought your pc, you planned to use it only for writing reports and managing finances. But then...

- You heard about the vast array of encyclopedias, newspapers, scientific journals, and other publications you can "read" via your computer.
- You realized you could save money by using your computer as a FAX machine.
- You became curious about the on-line forums that let you "chat" with people around the world.
- You bought additional computers for the office, and realized that connection to them would allow users to share programs and peripherals.

Welcome to the world of computer communications!

Computers and communications are natural partners. Linking the two has gained broad-based acceptance, not only among businesses but among educators, law-enforcement agencies, gaming addicts — indeed, people in every kind of occupation and with every imaginable interest.

There are two broad types of computer communications:

- Network communications: communications among two or more computers connected by cables
- Modem communications: communications between two computers via telephone systems.

There's lots of interplay among these types. For example, a person traveling with a notebook computer and a modem can access a network via a telephone. One network can communicate with another network, either via cables or via telephone systems. And people on a network can communicate by modem with computers that aren't part of the network.

LOCAL AREA NETWORKS

Local area networks (LANs) connect computers within an organization so that they can share data and resources. Some LANs have only two or three computers; others link together hundreds of computers. Most LANs are set up in a single building. But a LAN can extend through adjacent buildings.

Efficient   The rapid growth of LANs has been fueled to a large extent by the need to create, store, and move data easily and quickly from one computer to others within a corporation. Applications are infinite. For example, hospitals use LANs to connect fetal monitors in a maternity ward. This allows nurses and doctors to monitor vital signs remotely, from a central station, and to store data for review and analysis.

Cost effective   LANs offer computing power previously available only on expensive minicomputers and mainframes. Also, significant cost savings result from the ability to share expensive peripherals. Top-of-the-line peripherals become economical because computers on a LAN can be connected to and share the same laser printer, modem, graphic plotter, CD-ROM drive, and so on. Networks can be expanded as needed when a business grows, thus conserving capital.

The Parts of a LAN

Although LANs vary greatly in size and structure, they all have certain basic parts:

Hardware   A LAN connects computers, printers, modems, and other kinds of hardware. Typically, there is one central computer called the server. It's a combination traffic cop and librarian. It manages the information flow among all the computers and peripherals. Application software, databases, and documents are stored in the server's high-capacity hard disk drive and "served" up for you to use. Computers connected to the file server are called workstations.

Complex networks may have a number of servers. Basically, a server is a device, usually a pc, that handles special tasks. A print server allows users to share a printer; a communications server gives users access to a bank of modems; a computational server handles complex calculations; and so on.

In addition to having access to servers, a workstation may have its own central processing unit (CPU), memory, and disk drives. Or it may consist of only a monitor, keyboard, and mouse. This is called a dumb terminal. It can send and receive data but it cannot process or store data because it lacks a CPU and disk drives. It depends on the server for these functions.

Some LANs, called peer-to-peer networks, do not have a central server; control is not centralized in one machine.

Cables Devices on a LAN usually are connected by cables, which allow data and program instructions to be sent from one device to another. The most commonly used cables are:

- Twisted-pair cables: similar to telephone wire, with insulated wires twisted around one another; inexpensive; easy to install; suitable for short distances.
- Coaxial cables: similar to cable-tv cabling, with a central conducting wire surrounded by a copper or aluminum shield and an outer jacket; costs more than twisted-pair cabling but offers better protection against electrical interference and can transmit over longer distances.
- Fiber-optic cables: contain thin glass or plastic fibers that carry signals optically rather than electrically; expensive; not affected by electrical interference; extremely fast; offers better security than wire cables; can transmit over great distances.

Wireless connections are also possible. Some wireless networks rely on infrared light; workstations beam messages to one another along direct paths of light — but the data is lost if anything blocks the line of sight between the computers. Other wireless networks use radio signals, which can travel through wood and sheetrock, though not through steel or concrete.

WHO'S IN CHARGE HERE?

A company that installs a LAN should appoint a network administrator to manage and supervise the network. This person's responsibilities include such tasks as:

Performing maintenance
Adding users to the system
Monitoring the system's security
Assigning passwords to users
Controlling user access to files
Providing backup and recovery
Installing programs
Customizing applications
Improving network efficiency
Setting up training procedures

Software   A LAN cannot be run with a standard operating system such as MS-DOS or UNIX. Software known as a network operating system is needed to control the operation of a LAN. The network operating system works in the background, invisible to users. It directs traffic on the system. It enables a person at one workstation to access files that reside in other workstations, use a printer or other peripheral, exchange messages with other workstations, etc. The network operating system may be resident in every device on the network or it may reside in a server.

Many network operating systems are available. Some are designed for small networks, others for large networks. In addition to basic functions, the systems may have a wide range of additional features, such as:

- Internetworking features, such as the ability to tie together computers using different operating systems and the ability to connect one network with another
- Security features, including the ability to create and change passwords, and keep track of which users are accessing sensitive files

- Safety features, such as the ability to monitor the power supply, switch to a back-up power supply, and perform an orderly shutdown if the regular power supply remains off for a specified time interval.

Diverse utilities are available to handle activities and solve problems not addressed by the network operating system. There are utilities that report on the network's operation, improve menus, manage server resources, make files easier to locate, monitor security, and allow the network administrator to control the number of concurrent users of an application.

LANs also have inspired a new category of software called groupware. The primary purpose of groupware is to boost worker productivity by improving communications among employees and coordinating their activities. One such program may track projects, notifying people when their assigned tasks need to be completed. Another program may allow people on the network to comment on a report; they can suggest changes and read one another's suggestions without affecting the original document.

One final note on software: You'll want network versions of all applications that you plan to use on the LAN. The network version may cost more than the single-user version, but you save by eliminating duplicate purchases of the program. You also ensure that everyone will be using the same program, making it easy for them to exchange files.

Network interface card (NIC)   Every workstation needs a network interface card, or adapter, installed in an expansion slot. This printed circuit card connects the workstation to the LAN's cabling. It contains information on the workstation's location, or address, plus instructions for sending and receiving data over the network. Portable computers can be equipped with network interface cards so that people on the road can plug into their company's LAN via modem.

LAN Topologies

The layout of a LAN is called its topology. It describes how the hardware is connected and how information flows through the LAN.

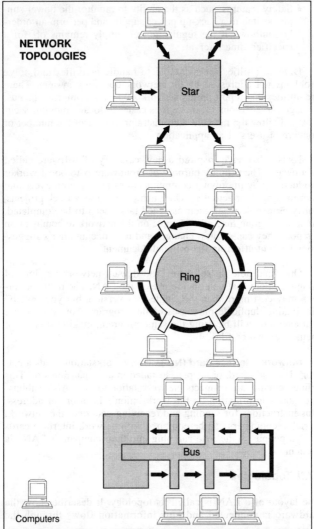

NETWORK TOPOLOGIES

Star

Ring

Bus

Computers

A message — whether a document to be filed or a note to another person on the network — isn't sent as a continuous stream of data. It is broken up into units called packets. Each packet carries the address of the device where it originated and the address of the device to which it is being sent.

There are three common topologies, as well as numerous hybrid arrangements.

Star topology   Workstations and peripherals are linked in a starlike layout; they radiate out from a central computer designated as the server. All communications are funneled through the server. This makes it easy to monitor the system. However, if the central computer breaks down, the entire network is disabled.

Ring topology   Workstations and peripherals are linked in a closed loop, or ring. Messages travel in one direction through the cable. Each data packet is attached to a pattern of bits called a token. A workstation checks the token to learn if the message is addressed to it. If so, the workstation copies the message and sends on the token, which now can be used to carry another message. All this happens at lightning speed.

Bus topology   All the workstations and peripherals are linked to one long main cable, called the bus. All data flow over that single cable. A device recognizes and accepts data packets addressed to it. If one device is disabled, the rest of the network isn't affected. But if there's a disruption on the main cable, the entire network is put out of commission.

A network laid out with a bus topology can easily be expanded. Two or more main cables can be linked end-to-end using a repeater, which is a device that strengthens a signal and passes it from one cable to the next.

OTHER NETWORKS

Wide area networks (WANs) use modems and the telephone system to communicate among computers separated by greater distances than those covered by LANs. WANs are popular among financial institutions. A bank with automatic teller machines in locations across a city connects those machines to a central computer via a WAN. MasterCard International has a worldwide network that is used for credit card authorization, electronic funds transfer, and other applications.

One day in the not too distant future, a high-speed national network, or *data superhighway*, may connect every home in the United States. The network, using fiber-optic cables, would allow computer data to be transmitted at speeds thousands of times faster than is possible over existing networks. Movie-like image and sound quality are planned, and the system would allow users to change data displayed on their computer screens and almost instantaneously send such data to other users.

GOING ON-LINE:
COMMUNICATING BY TELEPHONE

Millions of people routinely use their computers to communicate with distant computers via telephone. The process is called going on-line. There are numerous problems you can solve and things you can do by going on-line:

- You need up-to-the-minute information for a report on sugar prices, poison antidotes, or movie box-office receipts. On-line services have such information.
- You must send a contract across the country immediately. Electronic mail gets it there in less than thirty seconds.
- You're overseas, traveling with a laptop computer, and you want some data stored in your office computer. Again, it takes only seconds to make the connection and transfer the data into your laptop.
- You'd like to play chess with a friend who lives in another city. You can do this and a zillion other things.

What You Need

In order for your computer to "talk" with another computer, you need three things:

- A modem to connect your computer to a telephone line
- A telephone line into which the modem is plugged

- Communications software that tells your computer, modem, and telephone line how to work together.

The computer with which you want to communicate needs the same equipment.

Making the Connection

If you've never used a modem, the process may seem rather intimidating. But you'll get the hang of it very quickly. Then your only problem might be how to keep from spending every free moment talking with other computers!

Your communications program's manual and help screens will tell you how to enter all the necessary information. Most communications programs for pc's are written for modems manufacturered by Hayes Microcomputer Products, one of the first companies

---

DATA PROTOCOLS

Modems must follow certain rules, or protocols, when transmitting data. Both the sending and the receiving computers must use the same set of protocols. For example, modems send data either at random intervals (asynchronous communication) or at regular intervals synchronized by an internal clock (synchronous communication). In each case, various protocols govern exactly how the data are sent.

Microcomputer users are most likely to use asynchronous communications. XModem, YModem, and ZModem are common protocols for transferring files via asynchronous communications. Many modems can use any of these, while other modems use only XModem, which is the slowest of the three because it divides up and sends the contents of a file in comparatively small blocks. There's also an ASCII protocol, which can be used to transfer text files (but not files containing graphics). A good communications program will make it easy for you to choose the appropriate protocols for your work.

to make modems. When you purchase a modem, it's advisable to choose one that is Hayes-compatible. Be warned, however, that some modems that claim to be 100% Hayes-compatible do not, in fact, meet this standard.

To dial a telephone number and perform other chores, you must give your modem a series of commands. Hayes and Hayes-compatible modems use a set of commands called AT commands. The commands begin with the letters AT, which stand for "ATTENTION."

You begin by getting the modem's attention. Type (and press the ENTER or RETURN key):

AT

If the modem understands what you're saying — that is, if it recognizes that you want to speak the Hayes language, it "talks" back, replying:

OK

To dial a telephone number you use either ATDT or ATDP. The AT gets the modem's attention, the D tells it to dial, and the T or P indicates whether it should dial using tones or pulses. People with touch-tone phones should use the ATDT command; others must use ATDP. To dial the number 555-8237, type:

ATDT555-8237

Again, the modem will let you know what's happening. If it doesn't like the way you write a command, it puts an ERROR message on the display screen, and you have to retype your command. If the modem encounters a busy signal, BUSY appears on the screen. If it makes a connection with another modem, CONNECT — perhaps followed by a number — appears on the screen.

When a connection is made, you'll hear a high-pitched tone. This indicates that the two modems are talking to one another.

Before sending and receiving data, they must agree on how they will communicate. They must agree on four parameters:

- The baud rate, which as discussed in Chapter Two is the rate at which data are transmitted
- The number of bits in a byte; usually eight bits are used
- The parity, or the method they'll use to check each byte
- The number of stop bits; usually there's one.

On your screen, the information may look like this:

1200-8-N-1

This indicates that the modems will communicate at 1200 baud with 8 data bits in a byte, no parity, and one stop bit.

Or you may simply see:

CONNECT 1200

This basically tells you the same thing: that the two modems have agreed on how they'll communicate.

At this point, nothing further may happen unless you press the ENTER key on your keyboard once or twice. Then the system you're calling is likely to identify itself and ask for your name and perhaps a password. Once you've cleared its security system, it will probably present you with a menu of options and ask you to choose one.

Log On, Log Off

Connecting with, or gaining access to, a remote computer is called logging on. Ending the connection is called logging off.

It's bad manners to hang up on a friend in the middle of a telephone conversation. It's also bad manners to disconnect your modem in the middle of a data communication. Always use the proper procedures for disconnecting from a remote computer, following directions on your display screen.

ON-LINE APPLICATIONS

With your communications program installed and your modem turned on, you can truly "let your fingers do the talking." Connect with a friend's computer and start communicating! As you type on your keyboard, your words appear on your display screen — and on your friend's display screen. You also can send your friend a file.

Let's say you've written a report and you'd like your friend to comment on it. Send the report via modem and in seconds your friend can begin to read it and give you an opinion, ask questions, make suggestions, and so on. Later, when work is done, you and your friend can load copies of the same game into your computers and compete against one another, perhaps for the title, "Master of the Universe!"

Telecommuting

An increasing number of company employees spend all or part of their time working at home. Instead of communicating with the boss and other personnel by walking into their offices, they communicate via computer and modem. It's a great alternative to putting on a suit, going out in nasty weather, and spending time traveling on crowded trains or roads!

Salespeople who use portable computers while visiting customers can obtain information from their company's database, and send orders directly to the shipping department. Telecommuting also is used by many self-employed people. For example, a freelance writer may prepare an manuscript at home, then send it electronically to the publisher's computer.

Electronic Mail

One of the most useful and widespread on-line applications among businesses is electronic mail, or E-mail. An E-mail system allows you to send letters, reports, graphics, and other materials you create on your computer to other computer users.

Each user of an E-mail system has an *electronic mailbox* — actually, a defined space on a hard disk. You place your outgoing mail in your mailbox and type the recipient's "address," or account number. In seconds, the mail is in the recipient's mailbox.

The person can use his or her pc at any time of day or night to check for mail. The mail can be read from the display screen, printed out on paper, saved onto a disk, or all three.

Advantages E-mail gives you the ability to:

- Send letters, reports, and other messages in minutes or even seconds
- Receive confirmation within seconds that your messages have reached their destination (eliminating the "it must have gotten lost in the mail" excuse!)
- Send the same message to hundreds of people with a single command
- Save money; it costs much less to send a lengthy report across country via E-mail than via a courier service
- Send messages at any time, including at night when telephone rates are cheaper
- Avoid "telephone tag"
- Cut through an organization's bureaucracy by permitting anyone to communicate with anyone else, regardless of rank (studies indicate that low- and middle-level employees are more likely to communicate with a chief executive officer via computer than via telephone or written memo)
- Reduce paper consumption, especially for ordinary office memos and letters.

Types of systems Some E-mail systems operate within a single corporation as part of a local-area network (LAN). Others are public systems that operate over telephone lines and charge subscribers a fee. The latter may be part of a larger system, such as a bulletin board system or information utility.

Nowadays, most E-mail companies use an internationally agreed upon set of software protocols, known as X.400. This allows subscribers of one service to exchange messages with subscribers of other services.

Voice Mail

Voice mail, also known as voice messaging, is like a computerized telephone answering machine. You use an ordinary telephone to call someone with voice mail. You hear a recorded message from that person, asking you to leave a message. You speak your message into your telephone. At the other end of the line, a voice digitizer measures the sound frequencies in your voice and gives them values that can be stored in the computer as binary 1s and 0s. When the recipient plays back his or her messages, a voice synthesizer reads the binary digits and converts them back into sound.

A voice mail system has far more memory than conventional answering machines. Also, the system can handle many incoming

---

GET THE FAX!

Instead of sending letters and other documents via the U.S. Postal Service and by E-mail, many people use facsimile machines, better known as fax machines. The materials they send and receive are called faxes, and the process of sending something is called faxing.

If you have a computer, you do not need to also purchase a fax machine. You can use your computer to send, receive, and print faxes — thereby avoiding the clutter, cost, and potential problems of one more piece of machinery in your office.

A fax machine works with paper. It scans images on paper and transmits them through the telephone system to a fax machine at the other end of the line, which reconverts the image and prints it on paper. In contrast, computer fax transmits documents stored in your computer. If the documents are received by a conventional fax machine, they are printed on paper. If they are received by a computer fax, they are converted into computer files.

Computer fax is:
    Faster Transmission time is less than for a document from a conventional fax machine.
    Higher quality The printout at the receiving end looks better; there's no chance that the original document was misaligned or covered with specks of dust.
    More efficient You're probably creating the documents on a computer anyway; why go through the extra step of printing them out before sending them?

calls simultaneously, which means that callers don't get busy signals and aren't put on hold.

Voice mail offers some of the same advantages as E-mail. For instance, you can record a message and have the system send it to several people — perhaps your entire sales force or even everyone in the company, including people who are away from the office but call in periodically for messages.

Cost effective   Computer fax equipment costs less, telephone costs are lower, and you save on paper.

Computer-based fax requires both hardware and software, which often are sold together as a complete package. You have several choices. You can buy a fax board that you install in a slot inside your computer; an external unit that plugs into the computer's serial port; or an internal or external combination fax/modem unit — a particularly attractive choice for on-the-road computer users.

The main drawback of computer fax is at the receiving end. In order to receive a fax, the computer has to be turned on. Many businesses send faxes at night or on the weekend when telephone rates are lower. If your computer isn't on 7 days a week and 'round the clock, you could miss important messages.

Many people find it useful to have both computer fax and conventional fax — the former for sending, the latter for receiving. Manufacturers of conventional fax machines are now selling some models with serial ports so they can be connected to computers. This enables a user to send faxes from a computer directly through the fax machine.

Subscribers to on-line services such as MCI Mail and CompuServe have yet another option: send documents to the service. It will translate a document into fax format and send it off to as many recipients as you request.

Bulletin Board Systems

A computer bulletin board system (BBS), is much like a cork bulletin board. You can leave messages and you can read messages left by other people. But a BBS allows you to do lots of other things, too. You can "chat" with other callers by typing messages back and forth; play games with other callers; and download programs for use on your own computer.

A BBS consists of a computer and special software that allows other computers to connect to the computer via a telephone line. There are thousands of BBSs. Some are offered by commercial on-line information utilities that charge access fees. Others are free, though they may request contributions from regular users. The person who maintains a BBS is called the system operator, or sysop (pronounced "siss-op").

Most BBSs are organized around a particular topic. The range of interests covered is limitless: astrology, auto repair, computers, dating, employment opportunities, environmental issues, farming, games, geneology, ham radio, human rights, medical issues, restaurants, sports, used cars, and so on.

Many businesses and government agencies operate BBSs, some of which are open to the public. Here are some examples:

- A manufacturer's BBS provides technical support to customers
- A hospital's BBS lets people consult with medical personnel about nutrition, diseases, etc.
- A tourist bureau's BBS allows people to make hotel reservations and get information on weather conditions
- A politician's BBS surveys voter opinion on proposed legislation
- A university's BBS provides information on scholarships, student loans, and grant programs.

Some BBSs are open to anyone but charge a fee to users who want to participate in on-line conversations. Other BBSs can be accessed only by authorized callers. A company may use a BBS for communications between headquarters and field offices. An association may use a BBS to alert members to employment opportunities.

It's best to begin by calling a local BBS. This way, you can get the hang of logging on and off without paying long-distance telephone charges. Local computer user groups and computer stores often can supply a list of BBSs and their telephone numbers. Books on telecommunications and bulletin boards often contain lists, though the authors generally warn that the numbers may be outdated; because BBSs tend to be one-person operations, many of them appear and disappear very quickly.

Hopefully, your source of BBS names and phone numbers can also provide the parameters at which each BBS operates. The information may look something like this:

3/12/2400-8-N-1

This indicates that the BBS can operate at 300, 1200, and 2400 baud, with 8 bits, no parity, and 1 stop bit.

Your communications program's manual and help screens will tell you how to enter all the necessary information. If you don't know the parameters of a BBS you want to call, set your modem at widely used parameters, such as 1200-8-N-1 and see if you get a connection.

A BBS may have only one phone line, so it's possible that you'll get a busy signal. Even if the BBS has several lines, busy signals are common, especially in the early evening. If you get a busy signal, hang up and try again in a few minutes — unless your modem has an auto-redial feature that enables it to automatically redial a number until a connection is made.

Logging on When you've made a connection to a BBS, the first screen you'll see will probably welcome you to the BBS and give you some basic information about the system, including the telephone number, baud rate, and hours of operation. Then the BBS will ask for some information, such as your name and a password. Typically, all you need to do is follow instructions on the screen.

Here are two suggestions on passwords:

- Choose something that's easy to remember, or write it down for future reference

- To protect your privacy and for security purposes, use a different password for each BBS.

Once you have logged on, the BBS's main menu will probably appear on your display screen, with instructions on how to indicate the item you want to see. The best place to start is a file that tells you about this particular BBS: what services it offers, if it charges an access fee for some of these services, and so on. If there is a help file, you may want to print it, so that you can refer to it in the future. This will be faster than having to look at the file each time you need assistance (a particularly important consideration when you're calling long distance).

Next, you may want to read messages, and perhaps enter one of your own. Again, make the necessary menu selections and follow directions. However, don't try to do too much the first time or two that you log on to a BBS. Just get a feel for the basic procedures. As you become comfortable with logging on and off and with learning how to use the system's menus, you can expand your explorations, first within that BBS, then to other BBSs. Most BBSs work similarly, though there are variations in the commands you'll have to use.

Logging off   NEVER hang up on a BBS by turning off your modem or exiting your communications program. This can disrupt the BBS's operations. Always return to the main menu of the BBS and follow the correct logoff procedure.

Information Utilities

On-line information utilities — also known as on-line services and information services — offer a broad array of services that can be accessed by the public for a fee. Typical services include:

- Databases on general-interest and specialized subjects
- Up-to-the-minute news, sports scores, stock quotes, and weather reports
- Bulletin boards
- Forums where you can "talk" with other subscribers
- Electronic mail
- Electronic shopping for clothing, books, food, flowers, computer supplies, and other products

- Reservations for airlines, hotels, and rental cars
- Teleconferencing
- Home banking
- Games to play with other subscribers.

The costs of membership Fees vary from one information utility to another. Generally, there is an initial membership fee. Then there's a monthly charge, usually a minimum fee plus a fee based on the connect time — the number of minutes you are connected to the utility. The higher the baud rate at which you connect, the greater the cost. Additional fees may be charged for access to certain databases or services.

Choosing an information utility To choose the utility that best meets your needs, begin by answering these questions:

1. Why do you want to subscribe? Are you mainly interested in BBSs and chatting? Do you want to access scientific or business databases? Do you hope to participate in conferences with other people in your industry?

2. How much does it cost? What are the initial start-up costs? Monthly charges? Connect-time rates? Are there additional fees for certain services that you might use?

3. Does the utility support your hardware and software?

4. Does the utility provide introductory tutorials and other materials to help familiarize users with the various services? Are manuals complete and easy to understand? Is there an 800 customer support number?

Major on-line utilities Each utility listed here offers its own unique mix of resources. Some are more appropriate for home users, while others are geared toward businesses.

- BRS and BRS After Dark 800-345-4277
- CompuServe 614-457-8650 or 800-848-8990
- Dow Jones News/Retrieval 609-452-1511 or 800-522-3567
- GEnie 800-638-9636
- MCI Mail 800-323-0945
- Prodigy 800-PRODIGY

Some of these utilities offer gateways (connections) to other on-line services. For example, GEnie offers a gateway to Dow Jones News/Retrieval.

Using an information utility   Using a utility is much like using a BBS. One advantage is that you have manuals to guide you through the process.

Before connecting to the utility, review all the written materials you received. Make a list of basic commands, how to bypass menus to go directly to the services you want, and other essential information. Remember, you'll be paying for every minute of connect time; you don't want to spend the time trying to figure out what to do.

You also can minimize costs by doing your thinking, planning, and writing while disconnected from the utility. For example, if you are writing a report on tuberculosis, decide which of the utility's services you wish to access before connecting. Once you find the information you need, print it out so you can read it later. Don't spend connect time taking notes of material displayed on your screen.

To connect to the utility, turn on your modem and load your communications software into your computer. Set the baud rate and communications parameters, as described in the utility's manual. Then dial the telephone access number and wait for a CONNECT message. To keep costs down, call when rates are low.

You'll be asked for your name or user number and for your password. The first time you log on, you'll also be asked to provide information about the hardware and software you use. Then the utility will present its main menu and you can choose the options you want.

Chapter Five

BUYER'S GUIDE

There are dozens of worthy computer models, hundreds of nifty programs, plus numerous types of printers, monitors, modems, and so on. Costs for computers range from a few hundred dollars to many thousands of dollars. Some software is free while competing products sell for hundreds of dollars. How do you decide what's best for you? It may seem like a daunting chore, but actually it's not very difficult. With a little planning and the right approach, you can soon assemble the hardware and software that meet your needs and budget.

DEFINE YOUR NEEDS

Before doing anything else, you'll want to clarify why you're in the market for a computer. In addition to analyzing present needs, predict your future requirements. Here are some questions to answer:

1. Why do you want a computer? What do you plan to do with it? If you're going to be using the computer for letter writing and simple accounting, you won't need as powerful or costly a system as you would for professional desktop publishing or CAD applications.

2. Who will use the computer? Only you? Family members? Office staff? Ask other potential users for input concerning their needs. If children will be using the computer, find out what type of computer they use in school, and what software their teachers recommend.

3. What software do you (and other users of the system) need? Want? Which computers can run this software?

4. How much memory is required to run the software you want? A program that requires 2MB will not work on a machine with only 640K of memory.

5. How much disk storage capacity will you need? Will you need both a 3.5" and a 5.25" floppy disk drive in addition to a hard disk drive? This may be important if you expect to share disks with other people.

6. Where will the computer be used? At home? In the office? On trips?

7. Does the computer have to be compatible with other computers (in the office, at school, etc.)?

8. Do you need color and graphics capabilities? If so, what resolution?

9. What printing capabilities do you need? Do you just need copy for your own purposes or will you want to print classy-looking materials for clients? Do you need graphics capabilities? Do you need to print multisheet forms, labels, or 132-column documents? What fonts do you need?

10. Do you need other peripherals (mouse, modem, fax, joystick, plotter, scanner, etc.)?

11. How important is processing speed? Printing speed? Data transfer speed? If you expect to use the computer solely for home or small business applications such as word processing and spreadsheets, you don't need as fast a microprocessor as you would if you plan to do complex, large-scale graphics or professional desktop publishing.

12. How much do you want to spend? Develop a budget, listing all the costs of assembling a system (modem, printer, monitor, software, disks, etc.). Also list related expenses, such as finance charges, insurance for the equipment, office renovation costs, and training costs, if applicable.

COMPUTER SYSTEM BUDGET

ITEM	NAME/MODEL	PRICE
HARDWARE		
Computer	_____	$ _____
Monitor	_____	_____
Printer	_____	_____
Mouse	_____	_____
Modem	_____	_____
	_____	_____
	_____	_____
	_____	_____
	Hardware Subtotal	$_____
SOFTWARE		
	_____	_____
	_____	_____
	_____	_____
	_____	_____
	_____	_____
	Software Subtotal	$_____
SUPPLIES		
Printer paper	_____	_____
Blank disks	_____	_____
Mouse pad	_____	_____
Surge supp.	_____	_____
Dust covers	_____	_____
	Supplies Subtotal	$_____
RELATED EXPENSES		
Insurance	_____	_____
	_____	_____
	_____	_____
	Related Expenses Subtotal	$ _____
	TOTAL COST	$_____

SOURCES OF INFORMATION

Before doing any serious shopping, gather as much information as possible. Valuable sources include:

1. Friends and colleagues who own and use computers: They can let you try their equipment and software, provide suggestions on products that may meet your needs, and recommend retailers.

2. User groups: Local user groups are excellent forums for getting opinions on every aspect of purchasing and using hardware and software — from people who, like your friends and colleagues, have already experienced these processes. Often, meetings also provide opportunities to try the latest products.

3. Periodicals: Computer magazines carry reviews of new products and often do product comparisons. They also have zillions of ads, which provide useful price guidelines. Some magazines are dedicated to specific products. For example, *MacWorld* covers Apple Computer products and *PC Magazine* covers IBM and IBM-compatible products. Other computer magazines, such as *Byte*, are not product specific.

Also read publications that cater to your specific industry or occupation. Many such publications carry articles about how to incorporate computers into your business. They also review hardware and software, and may carry first-person accounts of how your competitors are using computers.

4. Retail stores: Learn what brands are carried by computer dealers, discount stores, and other retailers in your area.

5. Trade shows: Attend local, regional, and national computer shows, as well as trade shows geared toward your industry. They provide lots of opportunities to test equipment, pick up literature, and talk with exhibitors who are eager to explain exactly how their products can meet your needs. Often, workshops and tutorials devoted to specific products or types of installations are held in conjunction with the trade shows. Not only will you learn about products currently on the market but you'll also get a sense of what's scheduled for release in the near future.

READING COMPUTER ADS

As you gather information, learn the lingo! Familiarize yourself with the abbreviations, buzzwords, and acronyms commonly used in computer advertisements — and in salespeople's conversations. For example, machines often are referred to by the kind of chip used for the central processing unit (CPU) — an 8080 machine or a 486 IBM. Here's a translation of some typical advertising copy:

20MHz 386SX Desktop with small footprint   The central processing unit is an Intel 80386SX microprocessor or a compatible 386SX chip. The microprocessor runs at a speed of 20 megahertz; the model is designed to sit on a desk (as opposed to being portable) but it takes up comparatively little space ("small footprint"). Watch: the reduced space may mean fewer expansion slots or internal disk drive bays!

2MB RAM expandable to 8MB   Two megabytes of random access memory are installed on the computer's motherboard; additional random access memory can be purchased to bring the total to 8 megabytes.

130MB 17ms HDD, 32K cache   The computer's hard disk drive (HDD) can store 130 megabytes of data. The drive's access time is 17 milliseconds (the average time needed to read files or load programs). A 32-kilobyte area of memory stores the most recently used block of disk data, for faster access if the program requests that data again.

1.44MB 3.5"/1.2MB 5.25" floppy drives   The computer comes with two floppy drives: one for 3.5-inch disks that can store 1.44 megabytes of data and one for 5.25-inch disks that can hold 1.2 megabytes of data.

Internal 9600/2400 fax/modem   A fax/modem card is installed in the computer. The device can transfer a maximum of 9,600 bits per second but it also can operate at the slower speed of 2,400 baud.

1 parallel, 2 serial ports   The computer has 3 connectors where you can plug in cables: one for peripherals such as printers and two for peripherals such as modems and mice.

8 expansion slots, 2 occupied   There are 8 slots in which to install expansion boards for additional memory or peripherals. Two of the 8 slots are already used (perhaps for a graphics adapter board and an internal modem).

FCC Class B Approved   One of two Federal Communications Commission classifications for electronic equipment. Class B indicates that the item is approved for use in either a home or office setting; Class A is approved for office use only.

DOS 5.0 installed, Lotus Works   The price includes the operating system MS-DOS (version 5.0), which has been installed in the computer, and software called Lotus Works, which you can put on a hard disk or load from floppies.

LOOKING AT COMPUTERS

1. Bring along a friend who knows something about computers. If other people will be using your purchase, they should come along, too.

2. Take notes on each computer you're considering: whether it meets all the needs on the list you prepared, how the keyboard feels, the salesperson's name and telephone number, and so on.

3. Don't be afraid to ask questions or to appear "stupid." If the salesperson uses jargon that you don't understand, ask for an explanation. If the salesperson seems unable or unwilling to communicate at a level that's comfortable for you, find another salesperson or another store.

4. If you plan to use the computer to communicate with another computer, if files written on the computer will be used with another computer, or if you want access to a broad variety of off-the-shelf software, ask about compatibility. For example, can your child exchange disks between the computer and computers at school? Does the machine require modified versions of software? If you're looking at an IBM clone, check the BIOS (Basic Input/Output System) copyright notice, which appears on the screen when the system is turned on. If the BIOS was developed by a reputable company such as Phoenix or AMI, you can be pretty sure that the computer will run software designed for the IBM.

SHOPPING LIST

Before you go shopping, draw up a chart on which you can
compare data and prices for various systems. You also can use
the chart as a sort of checklist, helping to ensure that you don't
overlook important considerations. Include lines for the items
listed on your budget sheet, plus lines for such specifics as:

- Name of microprocessor
- Clock speed (MHz)
- Number of expansion slots, serial ports, and parallel ports
- Capacity (in MB) of hard disk drive and floppy disk drives(s)
- Type of graphics adapter (VGA, super VGA, etc.) and resolution
- Type of monitor (black/white, VGA, etc.) and resolution
- Operating system.

---

5. Try before you buy. Much like you test drive a car, you
should test any computer that interests you. If you'll be doing lots
of word processing, pay particular attention to the feel of the keyboard. If you're planning to use your computer mainly for financial purposes, ask the salesperson to load a spreadsheet program
into the computer, not games or desktop publishing. But also ask
about the machine's complete range of applications.

6. How do the keys feel? Is it easy to depress them? Too easy?
Are they quiet? If you're a touch typist, are function keys and
command keys positioned so that they don't interfere with your
typing?

7. Is information from the keyboard fed quickly into the computer, so that characters appear instantly on the display screen?

8. How much memory comes with the computer? Is this sufficient for the software you plan to run? Can the computer's
memory capabilities be upgraded? Is there room on the motherboard for additional memory or would you have to buy a memory board?

9. Look at the manuals that come with the computer. Are they clearly written and easy to understand? Are there a detailed table of contents and an index, making it easy to find information? Do the manuals explain how to solve common problems?

10. Ask about servicing. Where can you have the computer repaired if problems arise? How long do repairs typically take? Are "loaner" computers available?

Portable Computers

If you're in the market for a laptop, notebook, or palmtop computer, recognize that certain compromises must be made to allow for the decrease in size and weight. Consider the following factors in addition to those listed above:

1. Are the keys large enough and sufficiently far apart to be easily depressed? Are function keys, the ENTER key, and other command keys conveniently located? Located in the same positions as on the keyboard of your desktop computer? Such factors are particularly critical if you plan to do lots of typing.

2. Does the keyboard include a true numeric keypad?

3. How much noise does the keyboard make? This is important if you're planning on using the computer for taking notes in meetings or classrooms.

4. Is there a built-in pointing device or do you need to plug in a mouse if you want to run *Windows* applications? The former is preferable; there's one less thing to carry, plus it's not always easy to find a surface for a mouse while you're on a train or plane or in other travel situations.

5. What is the resolution of the display screen? Is it easy to read the display? Many portables have liquid-crystal displays that are illuminated from the back, making the screen bright and highly readable even in dim light. However, backlighting accounts for a significant power drain on a portable computer's battery, so models with a reflective screen can operate longer on a charge. If you're not planning to use the computer in dim light, the latter may be preferable.

6. How large is the display? Does it display the same number of lines as a traditional monitor?

7. Can the screen be tilted at various angles? Does it tilt back far enough to be easily read when you have the computer on your lap? Does tilting the screen back unbalance the machine, increasing the likelihood that it will fall off your lap?

8. Does the computer have an internal floppy drive? If you need one, you'll have to buy (and carry) an external drive. How large are external drives for this computer model?

9. What modem options are offered? Must you buy the modem from the computer manufacturer?

10. Will the computer run all the software you use on your desktop computer? Usually, this depends on the type of microprocessor, the amount of memory, and the amount of disk space.

11. Does the computer have built-in ports that connect easily to a desktop color monitor and to a full-size keyboard? This is desirable if you plan to use the laptop in your home or office as an alternative to a desktop.

12. Can the computer be connected to a local area network (LAN)? How?

13. How long will a fully charged battery operate? How long does it take to recharge the battery? How much does a spare battery cost?

14. Is the battery replaceable? How often must it be replaced? How much do replacements cost?

15. If you plan to take the computer overseas, you'll need a power supply that works for 100 to 240 volts. Is this built in? Or do you have to buy a power converter? (In either case, you'll need a plug adapter for the power cord.)

16. How sturdy is the machine? Can it survive the type of abuse it's likely to receive as it travels with you from place to place? Suggestion: buy a well-padded case in which to carry and store the computer, cables, disks, etc. In addition to protecting against bumps, the case protects against dust.

17. How much does the computer weigh, including the power supply that you plug into an AC outlet, cables, and any other items you'll have to carry around? Put everything in a carrying case and see how it feels to tote this weight around.

LOOKING AT PERIPHERALS

Regardless of what type of peripheral you are evaluating, you need to consider the following:

1. Will the model work with your computer?

2. Do you have an available port to which to connect the peripheral?

3. What additional equipment (expansion boards, cables, etc.) must you purchase in order to be able to use the peripheral?

Mice

1. What are the memory requirements for the mouse's software? Which operating system (and version) is required?

2. How responsive is the mouse? What is its resolution? Use the mouse for a variety of operations to see how it feels and how precisely it pinpoints items on the screen. You might also test trackballs, to determine if they better meet your needs.

3. How many buttons does it have? How many buttons are needed by the software you'll be using with the mouse?

4. Do you need a mouse pad?

5. Is it a *serial mouse* that plugs into one of your system's serial ports or a *bus mouse* that comes with its own adapter card? A serial mouse is easier to move from one computer to another. Do you have a spare serial port in your computer? An empty expansion slot for a bus mouse's card?

Modems

1. Is it internal or external? Which best meets your needs? For example, an external modem can easily be used with more than one computer, which is an advantage if you want to use it with both your desktop and your laptop. It doesn't use up an expansion slot in the computer — but it does take up desk space.

2. Is it Hayes compatible? If not, your choice of communication programs may be limited.

3. What is the highest data transfer speed supported by the modem? Does it also support lower transfer speeds? If you expect to send or receive large amounts of data, the higher purchase price of a high-speed modem is more than compensated for by savings on telephone bills.

4. If it's an external modem, how big is it? This is important if you plan to use it on the road — or if space on your desk is limited.

5. Does it come with its own software or must software be purchased separately? If you have to buy a communications program, be sure that: (1) it's compatible with your computer, your modem, and any other software you have; (2) it can save ("capture") incoming information that appears on the display screen to a disk or printer; (3) it can send and receive files according to established transfer protocols, including ASCII and XMODEM.

6. How easy is it to use? Do you have to flip tiny switches (DIP switches) before it will function properly?

7. If it's an external modem, what status indicator lights does it have? Such lights are among the important advantages of external modems; they enable you to follow the communications process, and help you track down problems.

8. Does it have an error-control scheme to cope with noise? Noise on phone lines can distort tones, causing the modem to interpret them incorrectly. Error checking is important if you plan to send data at very high speeds or if you'll be sending data such as medical records or financial statements, where an error can have serious ramifications. If the modem has error control, can the feature be turned off when it isn't needed? Also, is the error-control scheme compatible with one used by modems that are receiving your data?

9. If you're looking for a modem to use when traveling overseas, you'll need to find a model that will work with overseas' voltage. Also ask in which countries you can use the modem. First, the modem should comply with international communications standards established by the Comité Consultatif International Téléphonique et Télégraphique (CCITT). Second, some countries consider it illegal for a traveler to plug a modem into the local telephone system.

Monitors

1. What is the resolution? This is especially important if you need graphics capabilities.

2. Is it a color or monochrome monitor? Which best meets your needs? Monochrome monitors are less expensive and are sufficient for most business applications; color displays make it easier to use some software, and are essential for many programs, including most games. If you are planning to use Microsoft *Windows* you probably want a color monitor with at least a VGA and preferably a super-VGA card.

3. Will it work with the graphics adapter card in your computer? (A color monitor needs a color adapter, such as a VGA or super-VGA card.)

4. How many characters can be displayed in a line?

5. Are letters sharp and easy to read? Fuzzy images that are difficult to read can cause eyestrain.

6. Does it meet MPR 2 emissions standards, thereby limiting your exposure to electromagnetic radiation?

7. How easy is it to adjust controls for brightness, contrast, vertical display size, etc.?

READING MONITOR ADS

14" 1024x768 color A high-resolution color monitor with a maximum horizontal resolution of 1,024 pixels (dots) and a maximum vertical resolution of 768 pixels; the screen has a 14-inch diagonal.

.28mm dot pitch The dots used to make up the image are .28 millimeters in diameter.

horizontal scan rate 30 to 57Hz It will accept multiple horizontal scan frequencies generated by graphics adapters (from 30 to 57 hertz).

vertical scan rate 50 to 90Hz It will accept multiple vertical scan frequencies generated by graphics adapters (from 50 to 90 hertz).

tilt swivel base Allows you to position the screen at the best angle and tilt for viewing comfort.

Printers

1. What quality of print does the printer produce? Is poor quality (and therefore, inexpensive) dot matrix sufficient for your needs or do you require near-letter quality? Letter quality? Graphics capabilities? Color? Bring samples of the types of things you plan to print and ask the salesperson to demonstrate how they look when produced by the printer you're considering buying.

2. Can the printer print multisheet forms? 132-column documents? Labels?

3. What fonts come with the printer? Are additional fonts available on cartridges? Are downloadable fonts available?

4. What is the printer speed? This can be important if the machine will be used for high-volume printing or if you need to turn out work quickly.

5. How noisy is the printer? This matters if the machine will be used frequently or if it will be located near people whose activities could be disrupted by excessive noise.

6. How much memory does the printer have? If you'll be printing lots of graphics or plan to download fonts, you'll want more memory than if you'll be printing only text.

7. Does the manufacturer have a good reputation for high-quality products? This is particularly important for printers because they are electromechanical devices with a number of moving parts that are subject to wear.

8. How much will it cost to maintain the printer? What is the cost of ribbons? Toner? Other supplies?

WHAT'S INCLUDED IN THE PRICE?

Be certain that you understand exactly what is included in the price you're quoted. A magazine ad may show a system with a color monitor, with easy-to-miss type indicating that the color monitor costs an extra $399. A salesperson may give you a fabulous price but fail to mention it's for a stripped-down system with little memory and no mouse port. Here's a list of questions you should ask:

1. What hardware is included in the price?

2. How much memory is included?

3. Are all cables needed to connect the hardware included?

4. Is the operating system included? Will the vendor install it in the computer or must you do this yourself?

5. Is any application software included?

6. Does the vendor include a box of blank disks?

7. What is the warranty?

8. Are service contracts available after the warranty expires? At what cost? What is covered by the contracts?

9. Will the vendor deliver and set up the system?

10. What technical support is available free-of-charge? For a fee? Is there an 800 number to call for assistance?

11. Is training available? Free? If not, at what cost?

LOOKING AT SOFTWARE

As you begin to build a library of computer software, you'll quickly discover that products can be broadly grouped into three categories:

Commercial software   Copyrighted software that is sold by the developer, either directly or through retail outlets, and that may be heavily promoted by advertising.

Shareware   Copyrighted software that is distributed free of charge by the developer. It may be legally copied and passed from one user to another. However, if after trying out the software, you decide to continue using it, you are expected to pay a registration fee to the developer. The cost of shareware is less than that for regular commercial software, in part because instead of advertising it is promoted mainly by users.

Public domain software   Software that is available to the public free of charge; also called freeware. These programs may be copyrighted and protected against changes or commercial use. They are distributed through various outlets, including user groups and on-line bulletin boards.

Program Versions

Computer programs often evolve through a series of versions, each offering certain improvements over earlier versions. For example, a newer version of a word processing program may introduce a spell checker or allow users to work in a windowing environment. It's usually wise to buy the latest version of a program.

THE EVOLUTION OF MS-DOS

VERSION	RELEASE DATE	MAJOR IMPROVEMENTS
1.0	August 1981	first operating system for the IBM PC
2.0	March 1983	usable with a hard disk
3.0	August 1984	takes advantage of new 80286 processor, support for 1.2MB floppy disks
3.3	April 1987	support for 1.44MB 3.5-inch disks and 4 serial I/O ports, able to use partitions larger than 32MB
4.01	November 1988	graphical interface, support for large hard disks, expanded-memory device drivers
5.0	June 1991	better use of 80386 and 80486 processors, memory management utilities
6.0	March 1993	compression and memory optimization, virus protection, file transfer

The first version of a program is typically labeled 1.0. If the next version incorporates only minor changes, it might be labeled 1.1. But if significant changes are made, it will be labeled 2.0.

Generally, newer versions of a program allow you to work with files written using earlier versions. But if you're upgrading from an old to a new version, check to make sure that this is possible. Also, software producers frequently offer significant discounts on new versions to people who are registered users of their products. This alone is a good reason to send in that registration slip enclosed in a software package!

General Buying Tips

1. What are your needs? Will you really learn and use a high-power word processing program, or is a simple and less costly program sufficient to meet your current and anticipated needs?

2. What competing products are available that will work on your computer system? How do they compare in terms of features, price, and ease of use? Important: Make sure that your system has enough memory to run any software you're considering!

3. How has a particular product been received by reviewers? How is the manufacturer rated in terms of providing customer satisfaction?

4. Do friends, business associates, and teachers have recommendations? For instance, if you're looking for a program to improve your child's math skills, ask his or her math teacher for suggestions; the teacher should not only be knowledgeable about the programs currently on the market but also should know which would be most helpful to your child.

5. Is the documentation easy to understand? Does it clearly explain all the features of the program and how to use them? For example, does it explain how to enter special characters (ASCII codes 128 to 256)? This is particularly important in word processing programs and other software with which you may want to use Greek characters, mathematical symbols, or letters found in foreign alphabets.

6. How easy is it to install and use the program? Is an introductory tutorial included? Does the program have self-explanatory help screens or do you always have to refer to the manual when you have questions? If possible, test the software prior to buying it.

7. Have several versions of the program been published? Are you reviewing the latest version? Does the manufacturer have a history of offering new versions to existing customers at a reduced price? This is particularly important for programs in areas that may change rapidly.

INTEGRATED SOFTWARE

You can buy a word processing program, a spreadsheet program, a graphics program, and a communications program — or you can buy one package that contains all four of these functions. Such a package is called *integrated software*. It's usually much less expensive than buying separate, stand-alone programs.

The modules in an integrated software package use identical or very similar commands and conventions. For example, they may use the same pull-down menus and assign the same functions to the function keys. This makes it easier to learn how to use the software.

Typically, there's a common menu for all the modules. You highlight the module of your choice, then press ENTER to start that module. You also can exchange information between modules. For example, you can copy information from a database to a spreadsheet, do some calculations, put the results in a chart, then

8. Is the product sold with a warranty? What are the warranty terms? Does the company offer a no-questions-asked money back guarantee? Can you return a defective disk for a free replacement? For what period of time following purchase?

9. What customer support is provided by the manufacturer? Does the manufacturer have an 800 number that you can call if you need help? Do you have to pay a fee to have access to help? Are there special support programs for business customers who purchase multiple copies of a product?

BUYING A LAN

Setting up a local area network (LAN) in your business involves purchasing both hardware (cables, servers, etc.) and software (network operating system, groupware, etc.). Many of the criteria for buying LAN equipment are similar to those listed earlier in this chapter for hardware and software. However, there also are questions unique to a network that you need to answer.

place the chart in a word processing document. Yes, you also can do this using a combination of stand-alone programs, but not as quickly and easily.

Here are some questions to answer when considering integrated software:

1. Are the modules powerful enough to meet your needs? (Sometimes, you pay for the convenience of integration with less power and versatility in the individual modules.)

2. How easy is it to switch from one module to another? Do you have to leave one before entering another?

3. How easy is it to transfer files or parts of files from one module to another?

4. Is the software compatible with other programs you own? For example, can you take spreadsheet files from the package and merge them into your word processing program?

As you proceed through the planning and buying process, consult frequently with employees who will be using the LAN. If their needs are met, they will enthusiastically use the system. But if they find the system difficult to use or inefficient, their morale and productivity will suffer.

1. What are your company's needs? How many workstations will be connected to the network? Do you need something that works with *Windows*? With UNIX? Compile a list of needs and objectives. Make a list of all the hardware and software that will be part of your LAN. Note which items you already have, and which you'll have to purchase.

2. Which network operating system best meets your needs? Compare various systems in terms of performance, reliability, security, ease of management, and cost. Talk to people who are using the systems you're considering. Note: performance of a particular operating system may decrease as the number of workstations connected to the network increases.

3. What file systems does the network operating system support? Does it support DOS-to-UNIX connections? Macintosh connections? Does it allow you to assign passwords to resources? Can it retrieve deleted files?

4. Is everything compatible? For example, are the servers you're considering compatible with the network's protocol, software, and cabling? Is the network operating system compatible with the application software you want to use? Can the print server handle the number of printers you want to attach to the network?

5. Does the system support connectivity of products from a number of different manufacturers? Will the system be easy to expand or upgrade?

6. Are there network site license versions of the software you and your employees have been using, or will you have to switch to (and learn) new programs?

6. How easy is it to install the system? To maintain it?

7. What vendor support is available during installation? Following installation?

UPGRADING HARDWARE AND SOFTWARE

The rapid pace of improvements in computer hardware and software makes it tempting to constantly think about replacing current equipment with newer versions. But think carefully before switching over to something new. Yes, a newer computer may operate at 50MHz as opposed to your 25MHz model, but do you really need that extra speed? Yes, there are lots of "bells and whistles" in the latest application programs, but would you actually use those features?

Eventually, of course, it will make sense to upgrade — that is, to replace your current hardware or software with something that is faster, has more memory, or offers other features that justify both the expense and the time spent acquiring the skills needed to use the new purchases efficiently. If you decide to buy a new computer, think carefully before switching to one that is not compatible with your current system. It the two systems aren't compatible, you won't be able to use the software you bought for your current system.

Unless your computer system is really obsolete, you probably do not have to replace all of it. Perhaps you just need to replace that old 9-pin dot matrix printer with a 24-pin dot matrix printer or a laser printer. Or, if you're using a word processing program that doesn't work with *Windows* and you want one that does, you just have to buy a new program. (Remember: you may be able to upgrade at a reduced price to a newer version of your current program.) Just make sure that any new equipment or software works with your current system!

Here are some more ways to obtain added capabilities without discarding all your current equipment:

Replace the motherboard You may be able to remove the motherboard in your computer and install one with a newer microprocessor. The upgrade will run faster and provide access to more memory.

Install a RAM disk This is a memory-resident program that allows you to use part of your computer's random-access memory (RAM) to mimic a very fast, temporary disk drive. It also provides additional space for temporary storage, which is especially useful on systems without hard disks. However, because it's part of RAM, any data stored in the "disk" is lost when the computer is turned off or there is a power outage. (Note: newer versions of MS-DOS come with a RAM disk and instructions on how to install it.)

Install a high-capacity disk drive If you want to run bigger applications or store larger databases, you may find that your 20MB hard disk isn't sufficient. It can be removed and replaced with a hard disk capable of holding 80MB or more. Just make certain that the new disk is compatible with your computer's disk controller, which oversees all disk operations. If it isn't, you'll have to upgrade the controller, too.

Add a memory chip   For increased speed as well as the ability to run more powerful programs, you may need additional RAM. You can buy memory chips that you then install on the motherboard or plug into an expansion board. Since there are three kinds of RAM (conventional, extended, and expanded), you need to know which kind your system and software require or will accept. You also need to know the memory speed of your current memory chips; new chips should have the same speed.

Chapter Six

USING YOUR COMPUTER SYSTEM

When you acquire a computer system, you want to ensure that it will justify your investment by providing years of efficient, trouble-free service. You also want to ensure that the time you spend working with the computer will be productive and enjoyable. Meeting these goals depends in large part on how you set up and maintain your system.

SETTING UP YOUR SYSTEM

Even if you have never before installed a computer system, it probably won't take you very long to set up and connect all the unfamiliar equipment now stacked in boxes on your floor. The manuals that come with equipment today are usually well organized and clearly written, with step-by-step instructions on how to proceed. Follow those instructions and your system will soon be up and running.

Choosing Your Work Area

Before unpacking any equipment, choose and prepare the area where you will set up the computer. If the system is to be used by several people, set it up in a place that is easily accessible by everyone. The work area should be:

- Clean and dry
- Well-lighted
- Quiet
- Near an electrical wall outlet and a telephone jack (if you are installing a modem).

The desk or table on which you place the hardware should have a plain-colored, matte surface; avoid white or glossy surfaces that can reflect light and cause eyestrain. The desk should be stable and strong enough to carry the weight of all the equipment. There should be enough space on the desktop for paper, pencils, a telephone, and any other items you are likely to use while you're at the computer.

Place the desk out of direct sunlight, to avoid overheating the computer and warping disks.

Installing the System

As you unpack the equipment, make a list of all model and serial numbers. Keep the list, together with all receipts, in a secure place, so that you have them in case of fire or theft.

Remember, follow the set-up directions in the manuals. Perform all steps in the order presented in the manual. Proceed slowly and carefully to make sure that you put each cable into the correct socket, that pins in a plug are aligned with the corresponding holes in the socket, and so on. Each cable usually has different kinds of plugs on its two ends, making it almost impossible for you to make a mistake.

Do not plug in the power cable or switch on any component until you have double-checked every connection!

Save the boxes and packing materials. They'll come in handy if you ever need to move the system or send equipment away for repairs.

Power supply   Use an outlet that is on a separate circuit from photocopiers, clothes dryers, refrigerators, and other appliances that use a lot of electricity. Such appliances cause power fluctuations — "noise" — that could damage your computer or erase data stored in its memory.

Use only 3-wire electrical outlets, to ground the equipment, minimize electrical noise that could harm the computer system, and minimize interference that the computer system might cause to other appliances, particularly televisions and radios.

ERGONOMICS

People have become much more aware of the value of working in a "user-friendly" environment. Poorly designed work areas and equipment cause stress, tiredness, eyestrain, and other problems that affect health and productivity.

A science called ergonomics has evolved to study the relationships between people and their working environment, and to devise ways to improve the environment to promote safer, healthier, and more comfortable work. Designers and other professionals are creating furniture and equipment according to ergonomic principles. These include:

- More comfortable furniture, such as chairs with adjustable parts that offer good body and back support
- Monitors that can be tilted backward and forward
- Keyboards that separate the left and right halves of the boards
- Noise-damping hoods for loud printers.

Do not allow any part of your system, or any other object, to rest on any cables, wires, or power cords. All cables, wires, and cords should be placed so that they cannot be accidentally dislodged or tripped over.

Sudden increases in voltage (electric power) can damage computer chips, scramble data on disks, and wreck other havoc. Such *surges* often are caused by lightning or by the return of power after a power outage. To protect your system, buy a surge suppressor. This device sits between your equipment and the wall outlet. Plug all your equipment into outlets in the suppressor, then plug the suppressor into the wall outlet. If you choose a suppressor with an on-off switch, you'll have the added advantage of being able to turn all your equipment on or off by flipping only one switch.

A sudden drop in electric power can shut off your system, causing you to lose everything in the computer's random-access memory (RAM). Frequently saving work to a disk solves most of this problem (see Chapter Seven). Another solution is to invest in an uninterruptible power system, which uses a battery to maintain a constant supply of power going to the computer.

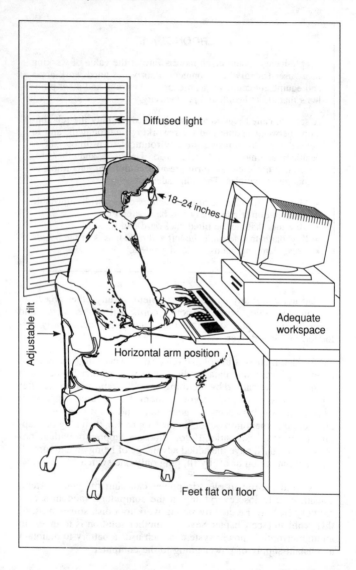

Diffused light

18–24 inches

Adjustable tilt

Adequate workspace

Horizontal arm position

Feet flat on floor

Ventilation The electrical circuits in computers and peripherals produce heat, which must be removed to avoid damaging the circuits and creating a fire hazard. Hardware has vents through which heated air can escape and cool air can enter. It is important that nothing blocks these vents. Leave space between pieces of hardware so air can circulate freely. Never place papers or other objects on top of the monitor or against the side vents of any equipment.

Lighting

Good lighting is critical. Avoid any lights that shine directly on the display screen and produce glare, which causes eyestrain. Windows should have blinds to prevent sunlight from hitting the screen or shining into your eyes. A glass non-glare screen or an anti-glare filter fitted in front of the screen can help relieve eye stress.

Experiment until you have the proper balance between close-up lighting and the ambient lighting in the room. Use a desk lamp with a hinged arm. Aim it so that it spotlights copy on your desk or in a copyholder — but so that it does not reflect light off the screen. If possible, outfit room lights with dimmers. This allows you to adjust the lights to achieve the most comfortable light level, both during the day and at night.

Position the monitor so that the screen is just below eye level — in other words, so that the center of the screen is at about the same level as your chin.

CARING FOR YOUR HARDWARE

More computer problems and costly repairs result from bad habits than from all other causes combined. You can help ensure that your system gives you years of trouble-free service by following these ground rules:

1. Keep your hands clean. Grease and other gunk gets in-between keys, sticks to disks, etc.

2. Don't eat or drink near your computer. Keep that coffee cup away! Many a keyboard has been ruined by a spilled drink.

TRAVELER'S ADVISORY

- If you take along your computer when you travel, keep an eye on it! Hundreds of thousands of small computers are reported stolen each year.

- At airports, request a manual check. Even though security agents will assure you that X-ray detectors are safe, too many people have had problems with their hard disks after putting computers through detectors.

- Carry a spare battery, especially if you want to use the computer on a long flight.

- Avoid leaving your computer — and your floppy disks — in a closed car on a hot summer day or on a winter day when temperatures approach the freezing mark.

---

3. Don't smoke. Ashes cause major problems when they settle in a keyboard. Smoke particles seep into the computer and disk drive, playing havoc with electronic components.

4. Keep pets away from your computer. Cat and dog hairs create problems if they get into printers, disk drives, disk envelopes, and other equipment. (Human hairs, dandruff, and upholstery and carpet fibers also have a way of creeping into equipment!)

5. Make sure that no papers, books, or other materials block air circulation around any piece of equipment.

6. Never move the computer while the power is on — not even an inch or two. Even slight movements can destroy data on the hard disk.

7. Turn off the system and pull the main plug if there are thunderstorms or any other signs of electrical disturbances.

8. Keep dust covers over your equipment when it isn't in use, especially the keyboard, printer, and disk drive. Be sure to remove the covers before turning on the equipment. (If you make your own covers, do not use static-generating fabrics; static can damage computer circuits and erase data on disks.)

9. Use an antistatic mat or periodically spray with a static guard to prevent or reduce static buildup on the floor near your equipment.

Cleaning Procedures

Putting off cleaning chores such as washing windows and vacuuming the kitchen floor may make your home look messy, but generally such procrastination has no serious consequences. Neglecting your computer, however, can result in a costly repair bill. Regular cleaning is important, and does not take much time.

For safety, always turn off and unplug your computer and all peripherals before beginning to clean hardware.

1. Check your equipment manuals for recommended cleaning procedures. For instance, the manual that came with your mouse should list recommended cleaning procedures for that device.

2. Vacuum your work area and exterior parts of the computer system, especially the keyboard and air vents, once a week.

3. Use a soft lint-free cloth or sponge to remove fingerprints and other grime from exterior cases. If necessary, slightly dampen the cloth with water and either window cleaner or a mild soap. Then, after cleaning off the dirt, remove any moisture with a dry cloth. Never use solvents or harsh detergents. Never spray window cleaner or soap directly onto the equipment.

4. To remove dust from the display screen, spray a small amount of window cleaner or special monitor cleaner onto a lint-free cloth. Be sure that the cloth is only slightly damp! You do not want any moisture to seep around the screen and into the monitor. Wipe dry with a clean cloth.

5. Yes, you can open up the computer occasionally and vacuum inside, but be very, very careful! You *definitely* do not want to hit a printed circuit board or other equipment with the cleaner hose or brush. A smarter and more effective method is to use compressed air to blow out dust, which can then be picked up with the vacuum cleaner. Compressed air, which is sold in small canisters by computer and office supply stores, also is useful for dislodging debris from keyboards.

6. Clean your floppy disk drives once or twice a year, using a special cleaning kit available from computer retailers.

CARING FOR FLOPPY DISKS

Huge amounts of valuable information are stored on your disks: programs that cost lots of money and data that took lots of time to enter into the computer. It's remarkably easy to damage this information. Avoid problems by taking the following precautions:

1. Keep disks away from magnetic fields, which can erase data. (Stereo speakers, tv sets, telephones, electric motors, magnetized paper clip dispensers, and electric pencil sharpeners are common sources of magnetic fields).

2. Don't expose disks to temperature extremes or sunlight.

3. When not using a disk, remove it from the disk drive. Put 5¼-inch disks inside protective sleeves. Store all floppies in disk cases to keep them free of dust.

4. Don't touch the parts of the magnetic surface that are exposed through slots in the case. The oil in your fingerprint can destroy data on the disk and mess up your disk drive.

5. Write on the disk label *before* putting the label on the disk. Place the label on a part of the disk where it does not cover any holes or openings in the disk jacket. If you must write on the label after it's on the disk, use a soft felt-tip pen.

6. Don't bend the disk or paper clip anything to it. These actions can cause warping or creasing, making it impossible for the disk drive to read data from parts of the disk.

7. Don't place books, staplers, and other objects on top of a disk. Don't stack disks one on top of another. Too much weight can warp disks.

8. If you want to mail a floppy disk to someone, enclose it in a special disk mailer (available at computer and office supply stores) or place it between two pieces of cardboard that you then tape together. This protects the disk against damage from bending. On the mailer or envelop, print "DO NOT BEND" and "DO NOT EXPOSE TO MAGNETIC FIELDS." Also, keep a backup copy of the disk's contents, at least until you learn that the disk arrived safely, with its data readable, at its destination.

WHAT'S WRONG?

Computer components have long life spans. Their failure rate is extremely low. But they are not invulnerable. Things can go wrong. If the system doesn't start, suddenly "dies," displays garbled messages, or does something else it shouldn't, don't panic. With patience — and perhaps some luck — you'll be able to correct the problem.

Diagnostics Many computers have built-in utilities called diagnostics programs, which automatically test components when you turn on the power. Other systems come with disks containing diagnostics programs that you can run when something goes wrong. You also can purchase separate diagnostics disks.

If a diagnostics program finds a problem in the system, it may alert you with messages on the display screen. For example, the program may tell you that a memory chip needs to be replaced or that a cable isn't connected properly. Other diagnostics programs indicate the presence of a problem by beeping. If this happens, turn off your system and check the manual.

Common Problems

Most common problems are not problems at all. Before assuming the worst, check for the obvious:

Nothing happens when you turn on a device Are all power cords plugged into live outlets? Are all power switches on? Are all cables properly hooked up and securely fastened?

A disk won't load Is the disk inserted correctly? Is the load level (in a 5¼-inch drive) down? Does another disk load in the drive? If so, the problem is in the disk, not the drive.

Nothing happens when you try to use the keyboard   Is the cable connecting the keyboard to the computer inserted tightly? Are the keyboard contacts clean? If only one or two keys aren't working, the problem may be a speck of dirt on the contacts.

There's no picture — or a weird image — on the display screen   Are all power cords plugged into live outlets? Are all power switches on? Are all cables properly hooked up and tightly fastened? Are the brightness and contrast controls adjusted properly? Is a magnetic field created by another electrical device affecting the display?

The computer doesn't work but the screen does   Are any error messages displayed on the screen? If not, turn off the system, then restart using your original boot disk. If that works, then the problem may be in your hard disk drive.

The printer is on but won't print   Is it off-line? If so, reset it. Is it out of paper? Are cables secure?

Suddenly, a program won't work, regardless of which key you press   Something caused the program to *crash*. Turn off the computer, wait a minute, then turn it on again and reload the program. While this will probably solve the problem, you'll lose whatever data you had in random-access memory (RAM) at the time of the crash. Note: despite its ominous sound, a crash does not hurt the computer.

Servicing and Repairs

If you cannot locate the source of the problem, even after reading the manual, follow these steps:

1. Call the manufacturer or your dealer and describe the problem to a service technician. Keep your fingers crossed: there still may be a simple solution.

2. Check your warranty. If problems arise while the equipment is covered by a warranty, it may be best to return the equipment to the seller or to the manufacturer according to the terms of the warranty.

3. If the warranty period has ended and repairs are needed, get written, itemized cost estimates.

4. Use a credit card when you pay for repairs. This gives you some leverage in case the repairs didn't solve the problem.

Some computer repairs are not difficult. If you're one of those people who delight in fixing things, check local libraries and stores for books on how to repair computers. Realize, however, that if you do try to do things yourself, you may invalidate the terms of a warranty.

ON or OFF?

It's time to take a break. Should you turn off your computer? The general consensus is that you should leave it on unless you don't plan to use it again during the day. The initial power surge when you turn on a pc is more likely to cause damage than letting the pc run.

Some businesses leave their pc's running around the clock. At best, this practice offers minimal benefits for the computers' components. But it's effect on electric bills is significant. At 8 cents per kilowatt-hour, it costs $105 a year to keep a 150-watt computer on all the time, but only $35 a year if you turn the computer off at night. Additional savings are likely as power management, a feature of portable computers, becomes common in desktop models.

Monitors are another matter. Unless you use a screen-saver utility program, it's probably wise to turn off the monitor — particularly if you have an older monochrome model — if you don't expect to use it during the next couple of hours. Leaving an image on the screen for an extended period of time may cause the image to be permanently burned into the screen. (Such an image is called a *ghost*.)

HEALTH CONCERNS

A significant body of evidence indicates that using computers is not risk-free, especially for people who spend many hours of their work days with these machines. Scientists have identified several potential health hazards. Fortunately, there are a variety of steps that computer users can take to avoid or minimize health problems.

Eye Problems

Eyestrain is the most common health problem experienced by computer users. The more time a person spends glued to the computer, the greater the possibility of eyestrain, perhaps accompanied by headaches. Research indicates that people who look at computer screens an average of six hours a day for more than four years experience difficulty in focusing the eyes, particularly on near objects. To prevent problems, physicians recommend:

- Proper lighting
- Frequent breaks
- Regular cleaning of the display screen to remove dust
- Annual eye checkups for workers who use computers for long periods of time.

Muscle Fatigue

Backaches and stiff necks are the second most common health problem, frequently decreasing people's ability to concentrate and perform at peak levels. To alleviate stress and tension build-up:

- Use a well-designed, adjustable chair that supports your lower back
- Keep feet flat on the floor or on a footrest
- Maintain good posture; for example, don't sit in a hunched position or with your legs crossed
- Frequently (every 8 to 10 minutes) relax muscles and shift working position
- Improve your ability to relax and increase blood circulation with both a regular program of exercise and periodic breaks at the computer to do stretching and deep breathing exercises.

Hand and Wrist Problems

People who spend long hours working on computer keyboards are susceptible to severe muscle fatigue and nerve compression — an injury technically called carpal tunnel syndrome (CTS) but also known as "writer's cramp" and, in days gone by, "washerwoman's thumb."

As tendons and other structures within the wrist swell, they pinch nerves that pass from the arm into the hand. At first, a person feels numbness and tingling in the fingers. If the problem isn't treated and worsens, the person may suffer from severe pain in the arm and shoulder, permanent nerve damage, and loss of muscle control. To reduce risks of CTS:

- Use a well-designed, adjustable chair and maintain good posture.
- Keep your wrists straight, with forearms and hands parallel to the floor; do not bend or twist your wrists as you type; do not rest the heel of your hands on the keyboard.
- Type with a soft touch; do not use more force than necessary.
- Take frequent breaks, switching for a few minutes to activities that use the hands differently.
- Improve circulation and strengthen muscles with hand, wrist, and arm exercises.
- Stop typing and mousing if you feel numbness or pain in your hand, wrist, or arm.
- See a physician if you suspect you have CTS; the earlier the syndrome is diagnosed and treated, the better your chances of a speedy recovery (and your chances of avoiding costly surgery).

Electromagnetic Radiation

Cathode-ray-tube monitors emit low-level electromagnetic radiation that has been linked with an increased incidence of certain health problems, including cancer, birth defects, and miscarriages.

For example, studies have shown that women who spend significant time before computer screens during the first three months of pregnancy experience significantly more miscarriages than do pregnant women who do not work with computers. It has not been determined whether this is caused by working conditions or by the electromagnetic radiation. One difficulty faced by researchers is determining what, if any, effects such radiation may have on living tissue over long periods of time.

To minimize exposure to electromagnetic radiation:

- Sit as far back from the monitor as possible; your eyes should be at least 18 to 24 inches from the screen.
- Sit at least 4 feet from monitors being used by co-workers (radiation is stronger at the sides and back of a monitor than at the front).
- Turn off the monitor when you aren't using it (reducing the light level does not reduce the amount of radiation being emitted).
- Buy monitors that emit reduced levels of radiation; most if not all new monitors comply with the MPR 2 emissions standards established by the Swedish National Board for Measurement and Testing.
- Unless color is essential, use a monochrome monitor; monochrome monitors usually emit less radiation.

COMPUTER VIRUSES

Everyone is familiar with the harm caused by cold germs and other viruses. There are similar "germs" in the computer world. They are pieces of computer code, rather than living microorganisms. But they share so many similarities with biological viruses that they have been named computer viruses.

Just as biological viruses can run rampant through a large portion of the human population, their electronic counterparts can spread among computers. Like biological viruses, computer viruses reproduce themselves and spread from one program to another. They may lie dormant for months or even longer, then suddenly attack hardware or software. And they are capable of wreaking incredible destruction.

Computer viruses originate with programmers who write the code. Typically, the code is attached secretly to exisiting software, such as a popular utility or word processing program. The program is then disseminated, perhaps via a company's computer network or an electronic bulletin board. Once inside a new host, the virus reproduces. It may infect any program on any disk used by the system.

At a preset time, the virus is activated. Some viruses are innocuous. Many, however, are designed to destroy or scramble data and programs, or damage monitors and disk drives. For example, one virus, *Friday 13th*, erases every program run on any Friday the 13th. Another virus, planted in one company's computer system, wiped out all records of sales commissions; the company lost 168,000 records before discovering and disabling the program.

Here are four important points to remember:

- Any disk may be infected with a computer virus.
- Viruses become activated, reproduce, and cause damage only when you are running an infected program; they do not cause damage when the computer is turned off.
- You can take precautions to reduce the risk of an infection, and to limit the damage that may be caused in the event that your system is infected.
- You can get rid of a virus, but if you don't destroy every bit of it, it will reinfect your system.

Trojan horses Closely related to viruses, in terms of meanness and illegality, are Trojan horses. A Trojan horse is a program designed to perform a secret function in addition to its advertised purpose — just like the "gift" given to Troy by the ancient Greeks. For example, a Trojan Horse may display cute graphics on the display screen while secretly erasing files on your hard disk. Unlike viruses, Trojan horses do not replicate themselves.

Worms Programs called worms do not infect other programs. They simply reproduce, making numerous copies that either spread from disk to disk or "live" in the computer's memory. When all these worms run at once, they greatly slow down the rate at which the computer can process your instructions.

VIRUSES ARE ILLEGAL!

People who write and deliberately propagate viruses are liable to be sued or jailed. Congress passed the Computer Virus Eradication Act in 1989. In addition, all states except Vermont have computer crime laws. The FBI has a National Computer Crime Squad that investigates viruses and other illegal intrusions into computer systems.

Preventing Infections

The chances that your computer system will be infected by a computer virus are rather small. Nonetheless, the possibility exists, particularly if you're part of a network, frequently use on-line services, or share lots of software with other computer users. Because viruses can cause extensive — and expensive — damage, it's wise to take steps against becoming infected.

A number of companies market anti-virus programs. These:

• Prevent viruses from infecting your computer
• Detect and eliminate known viruses already attached to your programs.

If you purchase an anti-virus program and run it each time you run a new piece of software or download a program from a bulletin board system you'll protect yourself against known viruses. Yes, many anti-virus programs are just like flu shots; they can detect and destroy known viruses but they may not detect unknown viruses. Thus you remain vulnerable to attacks by new variants of the disease.

When purchasing an anti-virus program, ask the following questions:

• How many viruses can be detected and eliminated by the program? Does the program rely on virus signatures, or does it use algorithms that enhance its ability to detect unknown viruses?

- What is the company's policy on keeping customers informed about, and protected against, viruses of the future?
- Does the program work on networks? Which ones?

Here are some additional measures you can take to protect yourself against viruses:

1. Buy software from reputable companies. Software from free and unknown sources is more likely to be infected.

2. If you use bulletin board systems (BBSs), stick with those that use protective routines to identify viruses and that restrict uploads to registered, verified users (giving the BBS operators the ability to track down miscreants). Many BBSs also provide anti-virus software that users can download.

3. Before you install a just-purchased program on your hard disk, close or cover the write-protect notch on the original disks. This protects the original disks from being infected by any virus that might be lurking on your hard disk. (Later, after you have dis-infected the hard disk, you'll be able to reinstall the program.)

4. Back up data files on floppy disks. Viruses can erase data files, but they rarely infect these files. If everything on your hard disk is erased, at least you'll still have copies of all your work.

5. Know the length (in bytes) of your programs. Periodically check the lengths, especially of programs that end with the file extensions .EXE and .COM. Viruses often append their code onto these files since they are relatively simple to infect. For example, a COMMAND.COM file may contain 25,308 bytes. If you notice that it suddenly has 42,851 bytes, it is probably infected. This procedure is not infallible. The Whale virus adds 9,216 bytes to a program — but subtracts 9,216 from the file size number listed in the directory, thus giving the impression that the file hasn't grown in size!

6. Watch for sudden changes in your computer system's performance, such as an unexpected decrease in the amount of space available on your hard disk, unusual error messages, or an increase in the time it takes to load and run a program.

Treating Infections

If a virus infects your system, you'll want to get rid of it as quickly as possible, to prevent futher damage. If you have a hard disk, it probably will have to be reformatted. Reformatting erases everything on the disk, so all those back-up disks you made suddenly become very valuable to you!

Your operating system manual explains how to format the hard disk. Just be certain to use a write-protected copy of the original floppy boot disk. After reformatting the hard disk, turn off your computer for at least one minute, to destroy any bits of virus that may be hiding in the computer's random-access memory (RAM).

Try to determine the source and extent of the infection. Use an anti-virus program to learn which programs and disks are infected. Check everything! For example, if you formatted any floppy disks when the computer was infected, it's likely that they too are infected. Getting rid of a virus is very time-consuming, but not as time-consuming as having to repeat the process because you missed an infected disk that then reinfects the entire system.

COMPUTER SECURITY

The possibility of viral infections is but one of many reasons why computer security has become increasingly important. If you're a school administrator, you want to prevent a student from having access to other students' records. If you own a store, you may not want salespeople viewing information on the actual cost of items. If you've installed a network in your company, you don't want competitors to use their computers and modems to log onto your system.

Here are some steps you might take to avoid unauthorized access to your computer system and to information stored on your disks:

1. Keep your computer equipment in a room that can be locked when not in use.

2. Put a lock on the computer's power supply. Provide keys only to people who are authorized to use the system.

3. Install a password program. Assign a secret password or security code to each person who uses the system; the person must type in his or her password or code before getting access to the system. Change passwords and codes regularly, including every time an employee leaves. Additional passwords or codes can be assigned for access to specific files. Again, change passwords and codes regularly.

4. Purchase a modem that verifies a person's security code before allowing access to files.

5. Use a data encryption program for sensitive data. Encryption scrambles the information in a file. A special password is needed to translate the scrambled data back into its original form.

Chapter Seven

WORKING WITH DISKS

Most people work primarily — or almost exclusively — with magnetic disks. They buy programs on floppy disks, load programs from floppy or hard disks, save data on floppy or hard disks, transport floppy disks from a computer in the office to a computer at home, and so on. Working with disks may seem complicated at first, but the procedures actually are very simple. You quickly learn exactly what needs to be done to work efficiently with these storage devices.

INTERFACING WITH THE OPERATING SYSTEM

When you turn on your computer, the first thing it is likely to do is run a built-in diagnostic program to make certain that all the hardware is functioning properly. If everything is fine, the computer will load the operating system. The operating system may be installed in ROM or loaded from a hard disk or floppy disk.

You cannot load any application software until after the operating system has been loaded.

If you are using MS-DOS — the most popular operating system for pc's — a DOS prompt appears on the display screen when the operating system has been loaded. The prompt indicates the letter of the active, or default, disk drive. This is the drive on which the computer will store and from which it will retrieve files unless you instruct otherwise. The prompt looks similar to this:

C:\ >

POPULAR OPERATING SYSTEMS

MS-DOS An acronym for Microsoft Disk Operating System, this is the most widely used operating system. It is the standard operating system of 16-bit IBM and IBM-compatible pc's. (It also is marketed as PC-DOS.) It allows a user to run one application program at a time.

Macintosh Operating System Unlike IBM PCs and their compatibles, the Macintosh can only support one operating system, which is built into read-only memory (ROM). The operating system is not compatible with MS-DOS.

OS/2 An acronym for Operating System/2, this system is designed for 32-bit IBM PCs and PC-compatible computers. It allows a user to run several application programs at once (a process called multitasking). It is compatible with MS-DOS.

UNIX A complex multiuser, multitasking operating system designed to run on a wide variety of computers, from pc's to mainframes. It is not compatible with MS-DOS.

XENIX A version of UNIX adapted by Microsoft for pc's and offering most of the advantages of UNIX. It is not compatible with MS-DOS.

Drive C typically is the hard disk drive; drive A is the floppy disk drive. If you have two floppy disk drives, the second one is drive B.

The prompt is the computer's way of asking you what you want it to do. You may ask it to load a program or delete a file on a disk or print a file from a disk. When the computer has completed the task, the prompt will again be displayed on the screen, awaiting your next command.

For example, let's say you want to change the active disk drive from C to A. Type A:.

$$C:\ \backslash >A:$$

As soon as you press the ENTER key, the following will appear on the screen:

A:\ >

FORMATTING DISKS

Before information can be stored on a disk, the disk must be formatted, or prepared to work with a particular operating system. On Apple computers, the process is called initializing. The formatting process:

- partitions the disk into a pattern of magnetic tracks and sectors where data is stored.
- sets up markers for the computer system to track the location of each file.
- identifies and marks defective areas; this prevents the operating system from later trying to store data in these areas.

Some companies sell disks that are already formatted to work with a specific operating system. But you can easily do your own formatting, following directions in your computer or software manuals.

Warning!   Formatting destroys any information that may have been previously stored on a disk. There are several steps you can take to guard against accidentally destroying important files:

1. View the disk directory before issuing the format command. For example, here's what you would do on a MS-DOS system if the active disk drive is drive C and you were about to format a disk in drive A: At the C:\ > prompt, type dir A:

C:\ >dir A:

After you press the ENTER key, the computer will list on the display screen all the files on the disk in drive A. If there are no files on the disk, a message such as the following will appear on the screen:

Directory of A:
File not found

This confirms that you can safely format the disk.

2. Always specify the disk drive containing the disk you want to format:

C:\ format a:

This protects against accidentally formatting your hard disk.

3. Pay attention to messages on the display screen. The operating system usually indicates the parameters you have requested and asks you to confirm the formatting commands, perhaps by typing Y for "yes."

LABELING DISKS

It doesn't take long for a computer user to assemble a stack of floppy disks, each filled with a number of files, or documents. If the person uses a hard disk, it may soon contain thousands of files. Without some pre-planning, locating a specific file can be a very time-consuming chore.

Think of that hard disk or stack of floppies as a file cabinet. Like the file cabinet, it contains lots of information. To be easily accessible, the information needs to be organized and labeled. With a file cabinet, you label each drawer. Then you group files into folders and label each folder. If a folder gets too big, you subdivide it into two or more folders.

On a computer you do basically the same thing:

- Label the drives
- Label the directories
- Label the files.

DIRECTORIES

A directory is a list of the files stored on a disk. Every disk has at least one directory, called the root directory. You can create subdivisions, or subdirectories, of the root directory.

As seen in the illustration, a graphic representation of this type of organization resembles the branching structure of an upside-

A SAMPLE DIRECTORY TREE

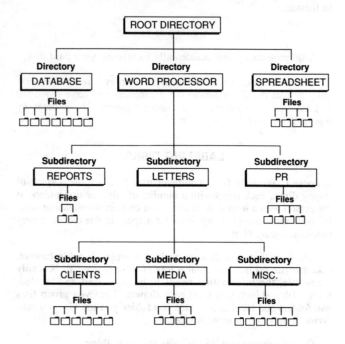

down tree. The top-level, or root, directory, branches into a number of divisions called directories. Each directory branches into two or more subdirectories. A subdirectory may also branch into two or more subdirectories. Each subdirectory holds one or more files.

Some systems refer to this type of organization as a hierarchical file system. But you're more likely to hear it called a tree directory.

Directories are essential if you use a hard disk, because of the huge number of files that can be stored on the hard disk. If you only use floppy disks, it's usually possible to keep files organized by putting them on different disks — for example, certain disks for files relating to the XYZ Corp., other disks for income tax files, etc.

FILE NAMES

When you create a file, you give it a name. This name should be unique and meaningful, so that the file can be easily identified and found. For example, LETTER and DATA are vague; they seldom are good file names. In contrast, IRS0690 is specific; it would be a good file name for a letter written to the Internal Revenue Service in June 1990.

The number and type of characters that may be used in a file name depend on the operating system. It's important to read the manuals that come with your operating system to learn what you may use. For example, MS-DOS limits the names to no more than 8 characters. MS-DOS also places other restrictions on file names. They may not contain spaces, commas, backslashes, or periods. Certain special characters also are unacceptable. For example:

Acceptable: DUCK(9A) DAD-MEMO RTE66   JBROWN
Not Acceptable: DUCK,9A   DAD/MEMO   RTE 66 J.BROWN

File Extensions

MS-DOS file names usually have an extension that helps you identify the kind of information contained in the file. The extension consists of a period followed by up to three letters: .TXT is used to identify a file containing text, .DAT is used for a file containing data, and so on (see box).

Files on packaged software almost always have extensions. For example, a file containing MS-DOS commands is likely to be named COMMAND.COM; a file containing information your system needs to use a mouse will be named MOUSE.COM.

As with file names, there are certain restrictions on extensions. It is usually wise to use standard extensions rather than creating your own.

Acceptable: 94TAX.DAT   ACT3.TXT   TRADE.US
Not Acceptable: 94TAX. DATA ACT3.<4>   TRADE.U.S.

COMMON MS-DOS FILE EXTENSIONS

Extension	Type of File
.ASM	program written in assembly language
.BAK	backup file
.BAS	file or program written in BASIC
.BAT	batch file (contains a list of commands that MS-DOS carries out as a set)
.C	program written in C .
.COM	command file (contains a program your computer can run)
.DAT	data file
.DBF	database file
.DOC	document file
.EXE	executable file (contains a program your computer can run)
.HLP	help file
.LTR	letter file
.MEM	memo file
.PAS	file or program written in Pascal
.RPT	report file
.SYS	file containing information about hardware (for example, the printer or mouse)
.TXT	text (ASCII) file

In many programs, if you create a file with a name or extension that's too long but otherwise correct, the program will simply chop off the excess characters. For example:

You write: MASSACHUSETTS.VACATION
The directory entry is: MASSACHU.VAC

If you later ask the program to load MASSACHUSETTS .VACATION, chances are that it will recognize the command.

WORKING WITH FILES

In a paper-based office, you can remove a file from a file cabinet and copy it, rename it, throw it away, or do a variety of other things with it. Similarly, there are a number of operations that you can perform on files stored on computer disks. Each operation requires a command. There are two basic ways to give commands to the operating system: text-based user interfaces and graphic user interfaces.

Text-Based User Interface

In a text-based system, you tell the operating system what you want it to do by typing in commands. Each operating system has its own unique list of commands, which are listed in the operating system manual. Here are a few common MS-DOS commands:

ASSIGN	used to assign a drive letter to a drive
COPY	used to copy the contents of a file to a new file
DEL	used to delete a file
DIR	used to list the files in a directory
GRAPHICS	used to prepare MS-DOS for printing graphics
LABEL	used to label a disk
PRINT	used to print a text file
REN	used to rename a file

Sometimes, the command is not enough; the operating system needs more information. For example, if you want to delete a file, you have to tell the operating system which file is to be deleted. Let's say the active disk drive is drive A and you want to delete a file named HAWAII.TXT on the disk in that drive.

A:\>

Type: del HAWAII.TXT

A:\>del HAWAII.TXT

When you press the ENTER key, the operating system will carry out your command and delete the file.

A command may require more than one parameter. For example, if you want to rename a file, you have to tell the operating system which file is to be renamed and what its new name should be. Here's how you would change MAY.DAT to JULY.DAT

A:\>ren MAY.DAT JULY.DAT

DISPLAYING A DOS DIRECTORY

Want to know what files are on a particular floppy disk or in a specific directory on your hard disk? Use a dir (directory) command. A list of the files will appear on the display screen. You'll see the file name, file name extension, amount of memory (in bytes) used by the file, and the date and time when the file was last saved to the disk. Here's an example of the command and the directory:

```
C:\>dir A:
    Volume in drive A is GROLIER
    Directory of A:\

    OUTLINE    TXT      30213      11-20-92      10:44a
    GLOSSARY   DAT     142542      12-05-92       3:16p
    REVIEWS             24209       2-24-93       9:30a
    CHAPTER1   TXT      18973       2-11-93      12:05p
    CHAPTER2   TXT      49652       6-18-93       4:57p
                      5 files              94950 bytes free
```

The prompt, in this case **C:\>**, indicates the current drive. If the user had wanted to list the files on the disk in drive C, the command would have simply been **dir:**. The **dir A:** command tells the computer to look on drive A. Notice that the person who created the files in this directory did not use an extension on the REVIEWS file.

On a hard disk with a tree directory, you also have to tell the operating system the path to the file. If the hard disk drive is drive C and you want to delete the file named SALES93 in the subdirectory REPORTS in the directory OFFICE, at the C prompt you would type

C:\>del \OFFICE\REPORTS\SALES93

Or, if you were already on the path

C:\OFFICE\REPORTS>

Then you would just type del SALES93

C:\OFFICE\REPORTS > del SALES93

Such commands must be given to the operating system — not to an application program. However, many application programs allow you to give at least some commands to the operating system without exiting from the programs. For example, a word processing program may allow you to tell the computer to print the file you're working on.

Check your manuals to see exactly how a command must be typed. It's easy to make mistakes. Leave out a letter, add a space, or type the wrong character and the computer won't understand the command. It will display an error message on the screen — such as BAD COMMAND OR FILE NAME — and you'll have to try again.

Graphic User Interface

Macintosh computers and computers that work with Microsoft *Windows* are among those that use a graphic interface. Instead of typing in commands that you must memorize (or look up in a manual) and spell correctly, you work with a mouse and a menu on the display screen. The menu consists of a list of commands or options.

With the pointer and a quick click you can select commands, manipulate files, and in other ways interface with the operating system. For example, to save a file, you might follow these steps:

- Move the mouse pointer to SAVE in the File menu shown at the top of the screen.
- When the pointer is on SAVE, click the mouse button.
- Move the pointer to the Directories list.
- Place the pointer on the directory in which you want to save the file, then click the mouse button.
- In a file name box, type the name you want to assign to the file.
- Check that all parameters are correct, then move the pointer to OK and click the mouse button.

Another advantage of a graphic interface is the consistency it offers users. It presents the same visual representation for applications as it does for the operating system. Thus, you follow the same steps to save a letter in your word processor program as you do to save a report in your spreadsheet program. You don't have to learn different commands and procedures for various programs.

WILDCARDS

As mentioned earlier, certain characters may not be used in MS-DOS file names and extensions. Among the restricted characters are two known as wildcards:

* An asterisk represents a group of characters.
? A question mark represents a single character.

Wildcards can be used as substitutes for file names or extensions. For example, by substituting the asterisk wildcard for a file name, you can find all files with the same extension. Suppose that you use an .LTR extension on all your correspondene. You want to know what correspondence files are on drive A. At the A prompt, type dir *.LTR

A:\>dir *.LTR

The computer will list every letter file on the disk that is currently in drive A.

The asterisk wildcard also can substitute for part of a name or extension. To list files on the disk in drive A that begin with the letters JFK, type dir JFK*.*

A:\>dir JFK*.*

But if you only want to list .TXT files that begin with the letters JFK, you would type dir JFK*.TXT

A:\>dir JFK*.TXT

You also can use the asterisk wildcard to copy or delete files. For example, if the active drive is drive C, the following command will delete all files on the disk in drive A with the name TAXES

C:\>del a:TAXES.*

Be extra careful when you use the asterisk wildcard in delete commands. Before you give such a command, know exactly what files on that disk will be erased.

If you wanted to list all files that have names of up to four characters, you could use question mark wildcards

C:\>dir a:????.*

There are a number of other ways in which wildcards can be used to speed operations involving files. Check your MS-DOS manual for details.

DOS SHELLS

To make it easier to interface with MS-DOS, you can install a program called a DOS shell. This program can be set up to run automatically as soon as the computer is turned on and the operating system is operational. Or it can be started from a hard disk or floppy disk. (Note: In version 5.0, MS-DOS introduced MS-DOS Shell.)

A DOS shell presents screen displays of directory listings and command menus. This eliminates the need to ask for a list of files, or to remember file names. The names of the files on the active drive are shown on the screen; you simply move a pointer or cursor to the program you wish to run and click the mouse button or press the ENTER key.

On one part of the screen are icons representing all the disk drives on your computer. By selecting one of these icons, you make that drive the active drive.

BACKUP COPIES

"My hard disk crashed!" moaned one computer user. "My dog chewed the floppies holding last year's tax data!" moaned another. "My kid used the vacuum cleaner around the computer and the cleaner's magnet erased half my disks!" moaned still another.

It's a fact of life: disks can fail — for any of a wide variety of reasons. When this happens, data and programs on the disks are destroyed.

Data and programs also are destroyed through simple human error. You may inadvertently format a program disk or delete a needed file. A co-worker may rewrite a file you wanted to keep in its original form. And there's always the possibility that disks and computers may be stolen.

To protect against loss of precious information, it is essential that you make backup, or duplicate, copies. The more frequently you back up your work, the less information you stand to lose. Your computer and software manuals will explain how to make copies.

How often should you make backup copies? To answer this, ask yourself another question: How much data are you willing to lose? Let's say you have a clerk who enters sales figures into a spreadsheet on your hard disk. If the clerk makes a backup copy of the data on a floppy disk at the end of each day, the most you'll lose if the hard drive crashes is one day's work. But if the clerk backs up only once a week. . . .

Backup copies of commercial software also should be made. Use an original program disk that you buy only once: to make both a working copy (perhaps on your hard disk) and a backup copy (on a floppy). This way, you don't lose your investment if you spill coffee on the working disk.

Store backup copies in a protected place, well away from dangers such as magnetism, freezing temperatures, and dust. To protect against threats such as fire and vandalism, keep a set of backup copies in a separate location. This is particularly advisable for such crucial data as a doctor's medical records.

In businesses that generate a lot of data, backing up a hard disk on tape rather than floppies is an attractive alternative. It's faster and less prone to error. Also, a single tape cartridge can store the equivalent of dozens of floppies.

THE SAVE COMMAND

You've been working hard at the computer for several hours, writing an important report. Suddenly, the power goes off. Did you periodically save your work to a disk? If not, you've lost it all, for it was erased from the computer's memory when the computer shut off. How do you feel?

You can avoid this problem by periodically using the SAVE command. This procedure is almost as important as making backup copies. It's a quick procedure, during which the file in the computer's memory is copied onto the active disk. Try to get into the habit of saving data every five or ten minutes. (Unfortunately, most people only develop this habit after experiencing the loss of some of their work.)

Automatic save   Many programs can be customized to automatically save files. For example, one word processing program allows users to specify an automatic save every ten minutes or every time 2,000 characters have been typed.

THE HISTORY OF COMPUTING

circa 3,000 B.C. The abacus — the oldest known calculating tool — is invented, probably in Babylonia.

1614 John Napier (Scottish, 1550–1617) publishes tables of logarithms ("logs") he invented, which simplify computations by enabling multiplication and division to be reduced to addition and subtraction.

1621 William Oughtred (English, 1574–1660) develops the slide rule, a mechanical device for making rapid mathematical calculations through the use of logarithmic scales.

1642 Blaise Pascal (French, 1623–62) invents the Pascaline, the first mechanical calculator able to add and subtract whole numbers.

1672–74 Gottfried Wilhelm von Leibniz (German, 1646–1716) invents a more sophisticated mechanical calculator, the Stepped Reckoner, which not only adds and subtracts but also multiplies and divides.

1801 Joseph–Marie Jacquard (French, 1752–1834) develops a way to use patterns of holes punched into cards to control the operation of weaving looms.

1822 Charles Babbage (English, 1792–1871) begins work on (but never completes) his Difference Engine, a steam-driven calculating machine.

1833 Babbage conceives of a programmable machine, which he calls the Analytical Engine, with parts comparable to those found in modern computers (input device, calculating unit, memory, etc.), and with instructions coded and punched onto cards.

THE FIRST PROGRAMMER

Lady Augusta Ada Lovelace (1815-1852), an English mathematician, documented the work of Charles Babbage in her *Observations on Mr. Babbage's Analytical Engine.* She is often referred to as the first programmer because she wrote a list of instructions to make the Analytical Engine perform, including such statements as "here follows a repetition of operations 13 to 23." She also convinced Babbage to use the binary system in his Analytical Engine (though, in fact, the machine was never completed). Perhaps equally interesting, Ada was the daughter of Lord Byron, the famous poet, though he had little direct influence on her life, since his wife sent him packing when Ada was only a month old.

1853 Pehr Georg Scheutz and his son Edward (Swedish, 1785–1873, 1821–81) complete a full-scale version of Babbage's Difference Engine. It wins a gold medal at the Paris Exposition of 1855 — the world's first computer prize. A version of the Scheutz machine is used by the British government to calculate life expectancy tables.

1854 George Boole (English, 1815–64) publishes a paper that describes much of his work on logic, which he reduced to a simple two-value, or binary, algebra.

1873 William Thomson (British, 1824–1907), later titled Baron Kelvin, builds a series of analog devices that draw charts recording tidal data, break down and analyze complex waves, and predict the time and height of ebb and flood tides.

1888 Herman Hollerith (American, 1860–1929) devises the first data processor: an electromechanical machine that can count and sort punch cards — the first such device to use electricity and the first to use punch cards to count, collate, and analyze data.

1890 Hollerith's machine is bought by the U.S. Government to process census data. In 6 weeks — one-third the time needed in 1880 — it determines the nation's population. The August 30 issue of *Scientific American* features the machine on its cover.

1896   Hollerith founds the Tabulating Machine Company. In 1911 the company merges with several others to form the Computing Tabulating-Recording Company, which in 1924 takes the name International Business Machines Corporation — known today as IBM.

1906   Lee De Forest (American, 1873–1961) creates vacuum tubes that can amplify electronic signals and can be used as switches for binary operations (an "on" signal representing 1 and an "off" signal, 0).

1930   Vannevar Bush (American, 1890–1974) builds the Differential Analyzer, the first reliable analog computer. Although mainly mechanical, the machine has electric motors that store number values as voltages in its thermionic tubes.

1936   Alan M. Turing (English, 1912–54) publishes "On Computable Numbers," a highly influential paper in which he describes a hypothetical machine with memory and processing capabilities that foreshadowed the logic of digital computers.

1937   John V. Atanasoff (American, 1903–) starts work on a vacuum-tube computing device that incorporates some of the basic concepts that eventually are part of all modern computers. The device, completed in 1939 with the assistance of Clifford E. Berry, is called the Atanasoff-Berry Computer, or ABC computer; it generally is considered the first special-purpose electronic computer.

1938   Konrad Zuse (German, 1910–) completes Z1, the first computing machine to use the binary system instead of the decimal system for calculations.

1939   Hewlett-Packard Company is founded by William Hewlett (American, 1913–) and David Packard (American, 1912–) to manufacture electronic test and measurement equipment.

1943   Howard Aiken (American, 1900–73) completes construction of the Mark 1, a 50-foot-long, 8-foot-high programmable computer that uses approximately 3,300 electromechanical switches to perform computations. It can perform 3 additions per second.

Scientists at Bletchley Park, a secret British installation, complete Colossus, the first fully electronic computer. The machine, which contains about 2,400 vacuum tubes, performs calculations at the rate of 25,000 characters per second. It is used by the British government to decode German military messages.

1945   J. Presper Eckert (American, 1919–) and John W. Mauchly (American, 1907–80) complete the Electronic Numerical Integrator and Calculator (ENIAC), a general-purpose electronic digital computer that can perform 5,000 additions per second. It was designed to calculate ballistic trajectories, but by the time the machine is finished, World War II is over.

1946   John von Neumann (Hungarian-American, 1903–57) publishes an influential paper describing the stored program concept (the idea that operating instructions could be stored in a computer's memory in numerical form rather than read into the machine from punch cards or perforated tape).

1947   John Bardeen (American, 1908–91), Walter H. Brattain (American, 1902–87), and William B. Shockley (English-American, 1910–89), working at Bell Laboratories, invent the transistor, which will replace vacuum tubes in computers, making computers faster, smaller, and more reliable.

1948   The first stored program — a search for the factors of a number — is run on the Manchester Mark 1, a computer built in Manchester, England. At one point, a moth gets into the Mark 1's circuitry, causing a malfunction and giving birth to the term "bug" as a synonym for all computer malfunctions.

A team supervised by Jay W. Forrester (American, 1918–) begin construction of Whirlwind, the first 16-bit computer.

The first efforts to use magnetic disks as a storage device are made, in an attempt to increase the memory capacity of EDVAC (Electronic Discrete Variable Computer), a machine designed by Mauchly and Eckert.

1949   Forrester conceives the idea of magnetic core memory and experiments with various materials before choosing ceramic ferrite. The first core memory was installed in 1953 in a version of Whirlwind built under the direction of Kenneth Olsen (American, 1926–), who in 1957 establishes the Digital Equipment Corporation as a mail–order parts business.

1950   Turing publishes "Computing Machinery and Intelligence," a paper in which he suggests that machines can learn and may someday "compete with man in all purely intellectual fields." The field of artificial intelligence begins.

1951   Eckert and Mauchly complete the Universal Automatic Calculator (UNIVAC), the first computer designed for commercial purposes and the first to use magnetic tape for input. The first model is used by the U.S. Census Bureau for tabulating the 1950 census.

While working on UNIVAC, Grace Murray Hopper (American, 1906–92) devises the first compiler, a set of instructions that converts, or compiles, a programmer's instructions into machine (binary) language.

1952   One hour after the polls close and with only 7% of the vote recorded, CBS-TV uses a UNIVAC to correctly predict Dwight D. Eisenhower's landslide victory in the U.S. presidential election.

1953   IBM introduces its first electronic computer, the 701. This vacuum-tube based computer has a cathode-ray-tube memory of 2K and can perform over 16,000 additions per second.

1954   IBM introduces the scientific 704, which can perform floating-point operations automatically.

The Naval Ordnance Research Calculator, built by IBM for the U.S. Navy, is the first to have a television screen display.

1955   IBM introduces the IBM 705, the first commercial computer to use magnetic-core memory.

The first computer for weather prediction becomes operational at Suitland, MD.

Scientists at RCA's David Sarnoff Research Laboratories develop the first electronic music synthesizer.

SHARE, the first formal computer user group, meets at the Rand Corporation in Santa Monica.

1956   John McCarthy (American, 1927–) coins the term "artificial intelligence."

1957   A team of IBM programmers headed by John Backus (American, 1924–) introduces FORTRAN, the first high-level programming language.

1958   At Texas Instruments, Jack St. Clair Kilby (American, 1923–) creates the first integrated circuit.

Control Data Corp. introduces the first fully transistorized supercomputer, the CDC 1604, designed by Seymour Cray (American, 1925–).

1959   At Fairchild Semiconductor, Robert Noyce (American, 1927–1990) and Jean Hoerni (Swiss-American, 1924–) develop the planar process, which uses photoengraving to connect components of an integrated circuit.

Hopper and others develop COBOL, which becomes the common language for business data processing.

1960   Digital Equipment Corp. begins deliveries of the PDP-1, the first minicomputer and the first commercial computer to use a keyboard (an IBM typewriter) and a monitor instead of punched cards; it has a memory of 4K.

1961   The U.S. National Institutes of Health Clinic Center begins using the first computerized patient-monitoring system.

The Massachusetts Institute of Technology (M.I.T.) introduces the first computer timesharing system; within a few years the concept becomes the fastest growing segment of the computer industry.

1962   American Airlines launches SABRE, the first computerized airline reservation system, to process a reservation in seconds rather than the 45 minutes previously required.

IBM introduces its 1440 series, the first commercial computers to store data on removable disk packs. The base model, the 1401, had a capacity of up to 16K.

At M.I.T., the first computer game is programmed on a PDP-1. Titled *Spacewar*, it's the hit of M.I.T.'s annual Science Open House; its popularity soon spreads to campuses across the country.

1963   General Motors produces the first computer-designed automobile part: the trunk lid for 1965 Cadillacs.

1964   IBM introduces its System/360, the first family of compatible computers, with all models using the same processing units. The computers are the first to contain integrated circuits.

John G. Kemeny (Hungarian-American, 1926–) and Thomas E. Kurtz (American, 1928–) demonstrate BASIC, the first general-purpose programming language.

Sara Lee, a producer of frozen pastries, opens the first fully automated factory.

1965   The first exhibition of digital computer graphics, arranged by three mathematicians, opens.

The first Ph.D. in computer science is awarded by the University of Pennsylvania.

1966 Operation Match, one of the first computer dating services, opens in Cambridge, MA.

1968 Honeywell introduces data preparation equipment that includes a typewriter-like keyboard to punch data directly onto magnetic tape, thereby eliminating the intermediate step of preparing data on punched cards.

Intel Development Corporation is formed by a group of former Fairchild Semiconductor employees, including Robert Noyce.

Using a mainframe computer, two programmers at M.I.T. write the first role-playing game (exploring mazes, fighting dragons, etc.); titled *Adventure*, it becomes a big hit among computer users on college campuses.

1970 The floppy disk is introduced, greatly speeding access to data; it is initially used to feed instructions to the IBM 370.

1971 Intel introduces the first microprocessor (named the Intel 4004). Developed by Marcian E. Hoff (American, 1937–), it has 2,250 transistors on a silicon chip less than 1/6-inch long and 1/8-inch wide.

1972 Intel develops the 8008, an 8-bit microprocessor.

Scientists at Bell Laboratories patent an experimental computer that transforms printed text into synthetic speech.

Magnavox manufactures the Odyssey 100, the first at-home video game, allowing people to play tennis, hockey, and maze games on their TV sets.

Atari introduces *Pong*, a ball-and-paddle game that becomes the first commercial hit of computer gaming.

1975 MITS, a small electronics company in New Mexico, introduces the Altair 8800, widely considered the first personal computer. Marketed in kit form, the Altair has 1/4K of memory.

William Gates (American, 1955–) and Paul Allen (American, 1953–) adapt BASIC for the Altair 8800. They later found Microsoft Corporation. By 1983, 40 percent of all personal computers are using Microsoft software.

Cray Research introduces the Cray-1 supercomputer as the fastest computer on Earth, capable of 100 million operations per second.

Homebrew Computer Club, considered the first personal computer users group, is formed in Menlo Park, CA.

1976 Stephen Wozniak (American, 1950–) and Steven Jobs (American, 1955–) form Apple Computer Company in the Wozniak family garage; introduce their Apple II computer at the Homebrew Computer Club.

1977 Personal computers are introduced by Commodore (PET) and Radio Shack (TRS-80).

Digital Research Company markets CP/M, which becomes the standard operating system for 8-bit pc's.

1978 Hayes Microcomputer Products introduces the first pc-compatible modem.

VisiCalc introduces the first electronic spreadsheet. The program changes the image of microcomputers, convincing people to purchase them for business applications.

1979 Micropro International releases Wordstar, which becomes one of the best-selling word processing programs.

1980 Texas Instruments introduces its first pc, the TI 99/4.

Pac-Man, created by Japan's Namco Limited, is introduced to the U.S. market. Pacmania sweeps the nation: it seems like everyone is playing the game.

1981 Commodore introduces the VIC-20, the first microcomputer to sell more than 1 million units. IBM introduces the

IBM PC, its first pc (a 16K machine using PC-DOS, an operating system designed by Microsoft). Osborne Computer introduces the Osborne 1, a 24-pound computer built into a briefcase — the first portable pc.

Ashton-Tate introduces dBASE II, the first popular database program for microcomputers.

Bell Laboratories develops an X-ray technique for producing integrated circuit patterns. The process greatly increases the number of electronic components that can be squeezed onto a chip.

1982 Compaq introduces the first clone of the IBM PC.

The U.S. Supreme Court begins using a network of 65 computer terminals to keep track of the cases it considers.

Jimmy Carter becomes the first former President to write his memoirs using a computer.

1983 IBM introduces its PC-XT, the first pc with a built-in hard disk drive (able to store 10 megabits of data).

Lotus Development Corp introduces *Lotus 1-2-3*, a powerful spreadsheet program that becomes a best-seller.

Nintendo Company Ltd. introduces the Family Computer System (Famicom) in Japan. In 1986 the company introduces the Nintendo Entertainment System — the first of a new generation of video games — across the U.S.

1984 Apple introduces the Macintosh.

1985 Commodore introduces the Amiga. Atari unveils the 520ST, complete with a CD player. Toshiba markets the first widely used laptop computer.

The desktop publishing era begins as Aldus Corporation introduces its PageMaker program for the Macintosh.

The Cray 2 supercomputer takes the lead as the world's fastest computer; it's capable of 1.2 billion operations per second.

1986 Intel begins shipping its 80386 microprocessor, a 32-bit chip that quickly becomes the brains of a new generation of IBM and IBM-compatible pc's. Compaq is the first to introduce a machine using the chip.

IBM announces full-scale production of the first 1-megabit RAM memory chip.

The U.S. enacts the Computer Fraud and Abuse Act, which makes it a felony to commit certain acts of fraud or theft related to computer trespass.

1987 Apple introduces Macintosh SE and Macintosh II. IBM introduces the PS/2 family of pc's.

IBM and Microsoft jointly introduce OS/2, a new graphics-based operating system that allows pc's to run several programs simultaneously (called multitasking).

Microsoft introduces Bookshelf, a collection of 10 reference works on a single CD-ROM.

1988 NeXT, Inc., founded by Steven Jobs after he left Apple, unveils a "computer workstation" featuring an optical disk drive capable of storing 250 times as much data as floppy

---

NEW CHIP ON THE BLOCK

The amount of circuitry that can be etched onto a silicon chip about the size of a fingernail keeps growing, leading to enormous increases in computing power. Ten years prior to Intel's 1986 introduction of the 80386 microprocessor, a similarly powerful device would have filled a room large enough to accommodate 2,000 people! The transistors on the 80386 are so tiny that more than 100 of them could fit across one human hair. They're just as fast as they are tiny. If the working speed the 80386 were slowed to the rate of a human heartbeat, it would take the 80386 one year to do the work that it normally accomplishes in one second.

disks; the machine is intended primarily for use in university education.

Computer scientists at Sandia National Laboratories develop a way to break down complex problems into tiny pieces so that they can be processed simultaneously by an array of inexpensive microprocessors; speeds problem solution by a factor of 1000.

1989   Intel introduces the 80486 microprocessor, a 32-bit chip containing more than 1 million transistors and able to address 64 gigabytes of main memory directly. It also introduces the 80860 chip, a microprocessor based on Reduced Instruction Set Computing (RISC) architecture.

GRiD Systems pioneers the notebook computer market with its introduction of GRiDPad.

1990   Scientists at Bell Laboratories unveil an experimental computer that uses photons, the fundamental partricles of light, rather than electronic signals, to process data.

Hitachi announces a working prototype of the first 64-megabit memory chip.

Sony and Canon begin selling battery-operated pen-based computers in which users write on touch-sensitive screens.

IBM introduces a line of nine RISC workstations, which are shown to solve certain scientific problems faster than even the most powerful supercomputers.

1991   Hewlett-Packard begins selling an IBM-compatible palmtop computer that weighs only 11 ounces yet has a built-in spreadsheet program, text editor, and communications link. It is powered by two AA batteries.

Thinking Machines Inc. introduces a massively parallel supercomputer that can perform 9.03 billion calculations per second.

1992 Hewlett-Packard introduces a 1.3-inch disk that holds up to 21.4 megabytes of information.

1993 Japan's Advanced Telecommunications Research Institute International demonstrates a test system that can automatically translate an overseas telephone conversation. In Kyoto, Japan, a researcher says "moshimoshi" into a microphone; 12 seconds later in Pittsburgh, PA, a computer voice conveys the message in English: "hello."

THEN AND NOW

	ENIAC	Typical 80386 desktop
YEAR INTRODUCED	*1946*	*1990*
DIMENSIONS	80' long x 8' high	5" high x 17" wide x 16" deep
WEIGHT	60,000 lbs	22 lbs
CIRCUITRY	18,000 vacuum tubes	32-bit microprocessor
POWER REQUIRED	130 kilowatts	0.2 kilowatt
PROGRAMMING	hand set 6,000 dials and switches	type in
INTERNAL MEMORY	100 bytes (.1KB)	up to 16MB RAM + 128KB ROM
INPUT	punch cards	keyboard, mouse, disk, modem, scanner, etc.
OUTPUT	punch cards	monitor, printer, disk, modem
STORAGE	none	80 MB hard disk + 1.44 MB floppies
GRAPHICS	none	800 x 600 pixel resolution with 16 colors

GLOSSARY

Understanding computerese isn't always easy, even for people with lots of experience in using computers. Frequently, a variety of terms are used to represent the same concept, process, or object. For example, *external storage*, *secondary storage*, *mass storage*, and *auxiliary storage* are synonyms used to refer to disk drives and other devices used for long-term storage of information. In other cases, words are used synonymously even though that may not be technically accurate. *External memory*, *secondary memory*, and *accessory memory* technically refer to memory stored on disks and other external storage devices — but you'll hear and see these terms used as synonyms for the devices themselves.

The widespread use of acronyms can provide yet another stumbling block. *OCR* refers to both a process (optical character recognition) and the device used in the process (optical character reader). *AC* is shorthand for *alternating current* as well as for *acoustic coupler*.

On the plus side is the fact that most computer terms are obvious, logical names for the concepts, processes, or objects they define. What, for example, could better describe the part of a computer that processes data than the name *central processing unit*? So don't feel overwhelmed by what at first is an unfamiliar vocabulary. Before long, you'll sound — and feel — like an expert as you toss around phrases such as *40-meg hard drive*, *132 cps*, and *high-res raster display*!

A

abort To stop running a program or procedure while it is in progress rather than waiting for it to conclude naturally; usually done when something goes wrong that cannot be corrected while the program or procedure is in progress.

AC (1) alternating current. (2) *see* acoustic coupler.

accelerator board An expansion board that contains circuitry to speed up the computer's operation.

access To retrieve data from a storage device.

access control The use of security techniques that limit access to a computer system or software to identified, authenticated users.

accessory A device designed to make a computer system operate more efficiently, or to increase the user's comfort; for example, document holders, dust covers, surge protectors.

access time The amount of time needed for data to be located on a storage device (such as a disk) and transferred to the computer's memory, where it can be used; generally measured in milliseconds.

accumulator A temporary memory location within the arithmetic/logic unit of the central processing unit (CPU); used to perform arithmetic operations.

acoustic coupler (AC) An external modem that does not plug directly into a phone line. Rather, the user places the phone receiver into two rubber cups on the modem; data from the user's computer goes out the mouthpiece and incoming data is received in the earpiece.

active drive *see* default drive.

active window In a windowing environment, the window in which the next action will take place (unless the next command selects another window).

ADA A high-level programming language named after Lady Ada Lovelace ("the first programmer") and used by the U.S. Department of Defense.

address (1) A specific, identifiable location in a computer's memory. (2) The name or number that identifies where specific information is stored in a computer's memory. (3) On an electronic spreadsheet, the location of a cell, identified by the column letter and row number.

adventure games A major type of game software, often text-based, that involves analyzing a situation, discovering the rules that govern the environment, and developing strategies to attain a goal (such as rescuing a maiden imprisoned in a mad duke's castle)

AI *see* artificial intelligence.

ALGOL An acronym for ALGOrithmic Language; a high-level programming language particularly suited for scientific and mathematical projects.

algorithm A precise step-by-step sequence of instructions (rather like those of a cookbook recipe) that solves a well-defined problem. Computer programs embody algorithms, which define how the programs work.

alphanumeric Contraction of alphabetic-numeric; letters and numbers.

Alt key A key on the keyboard that is used by many application programs to handle commands. For example, in some word processing programs, pressing I while holding down the Alt key will produce *italic type*.

ALU *see* arithmetic and logic unit.

American National Standards Institute (ANSI) A non-governmental organization in the United States that develops industry standards, such as those for programming languages and database management systems.

analog Composed of, or using, continuously changing physical quantities; *contrasts with* digital.

analog computer A computer that performs calculations based on continuously changing physical quantities, such as voltage or temperature; widely used in science and industry to monitor and record on-going changes; *contrasts with* digital computer, which handles data in the form of discrete binary numbers.

analog-to-digital conversion The process of converting a continuously varying signal into a signal composed of discrete numbers, so that the information can be processed by a digital computer.

analog tansmission The transmission of a continous signal varied by amplification, as opposed to a signal composed of discrete pulses.

ANSI *see* American National Standards Institute.

antiglare filter An accessory that fits over a monitor screen and protects the user against reflections and glare produced by the monitor. Some monitors are treated to provide antiglare protection; in other cases, a filter is desirable to help prevent eyestrain.

antivirus program *see* vaccine.

APL An acronym for A Programming Language; a high-level programming language particularly suited for mathematical applications.

application program A computer program that performs a specific task or series of tasks; examples include word processing programs, spreadsheet programs, inventory-control software, and computer games.

arcade games A major type of game software, similar to the games found in arcades; stress hand-eye coordination and have several levels of speed and complexity; examples include road races and shoot 'em ups.

architecture The overall design of a computer system, including how the various components are connected both physically and functionally; comparable to the architecture of a building.

arithmetic and logic unit (ALU) The part of the central processing unit (CPU) in which all arithmetic and logical operations take place.

arithmetic operations Operations that involve adding, subtracting, multiplying, and dividing.

ARPANET A wide area network sponsored by the U.S. Department of Defense Advanced Research Projects Agency that links computers at research centers around the United States.

array An organized collection of data that contains a number of elements of the same type; for example, a table of numbers.

arrow keys *see* cursor control keys.

artificial intelligence (AI) An area of study concerned with the development of computers that are able to perform functions normally associated with human intelligence, such as learning and reasoning.

artificial reality *see* virtual reality.

ASCII An acronym for American Standard Code for Information Interchange; pronounced "ass-key"; a standard code used by virtually all computers. ASCII uses 8-bit binary numbers to electronically represent letters, numbers, and other characters that a computer can produce.

ASCII file A file that consists entirely of standard ASCII characters; also called a text file.

assembler A computer program used by programmers to translate programs written in assembly language into machine language, which can be understood by the computer's central processing unit (CPU). The resulting machine code is saved as a program file ready to be run at any time.

assembly language A programming language in which each statement translates into one machine language instruction, as contrasted with high-level languages (BASIC, COBOL, etc.) in which each statement generally translates into many machine language instructions. Programs written in assembly language often are designed to be used only on one specific microprocessor or model of computer.

asynchronous communication The transmission of data one bit after another, with a start bit and a stop bit marking the beginning and end of each data unit; data are not transmitted at regular intervals timed to synchronize with the modem clock of the host computer; *contrasts with* synchronous communication.

attenuation The gradual dilution of an electrical signal as it is transmitted; usually measured in decibels. This is a critical issue in networking: one advantage of fiber optic cable over coaxial cable is that it offers less attenuation.

audit trail A record of transactions, accesses to data, or other specific events within a computer system; valuable in locating the origin of errors, detecting attempts to violate the security of the system, etc.

authoring system In multimedia, software used for creating smooth presentations by specifying how text, graphic, video, and sound elements are to be linked together.

auto-answer A feature on some modems that enables them to automatically answer ("pick up") a telephone after a programmed number of rings.

auto-dialer A feature on some modems that enables them to automatically dial a telephone number typed into the computer's communications program.

automatic save *see* timed backup.

auto-redial A feature on some modems that enables them to automatically redial a telephone number until a connection is made.

auxiliary storage *see* secondary storage.

B

backup copy A duplicate copy of a program or file, made to protect against loss of data; backup copies should not be made on the same disk or tape holding the original data (i.e., the master disk or tape).

badge reader A device designed to read information (such as employee name and number) encoded into a badge-like card, and then enter that data into a computer.

bar code A set of printed parallel lines of various thicknesses separated by spaces of various widths; represents data that can be read by an input device such as a scanner. An example is the Universal Product Code (UPC) used in the United States to identify groceries and other consumer products.

bar code scanner An input device that optically scans bar codes and converts them into a digital format readable by a computer.

base The number used to define a number system. In the binary system, the base is 2; in the decimal system, the base is 10; in the hexadecimal system, the base is 16.

BASIC An acronym for Beginner's All Purpose Symbolic Instruction Code; a comparatively easy-to-learn, high-level programming language.

batch A group of similar documents or records, such as a store's sales receipts or credit application forms.

batch file In MS-DOS, a file containing commands that tell the operating system to perform a "batch" of common tasks; indicated with the file extension BAT. For example, an AUTO-EXEC.BAT file contains a list of commands that a user wants MS-DOS to execute automatically each time the system starts up.

batch processing A method of processing data; data are assembled into batches, stored, and then processed at one time; used to carry out the same computations on a large group of similar records — for example, bank deposit slips; *contrasts with* continuous processing.

baud rate The rate at which data are transmitted between two computers connected by modems; typically measured in bits per second; for example, a modem running at 2,400 baud transfers data at the rate of 2,400 bits per second.

BBS *see* bulletin board system.

benchmark A test or series of tests used to judge the performance of computer hardware or software.

Bernoulli box A storage device that uses a very fast tape drive to store large quantities of data; used primarily in businesses to back up data from hard disks.

beta test A test of a software package by a small number of people outside the company that developed the software, to detect errors; takes place following extensive testing at the development site (alpha test) and prior to introducing the software to the general market. Beta testers usually are people who would normally use the software; for example, accountants would be asked to test an accounting package while teenage game aficionados would try out game software.

binary code A code using only two elements: 0 and 1.

binary numbers Numbers used in the binary (base 2) numbering system, composed of the digits 0 and 1.

binary system A numbering system in which all numbers are expressed as combinations of only two digits: 0 and 1; used in computers because the two digits can represent the on-off states of electrical devices.

BIOS An acronym for Basic Input/Output System; programs within read-only memory (ROM) of IBM PC and PC-compatible computers that facilitate input and output operations, such as transferring data from the keyboard to the computer or from the computer to a disk drive.

bit A contraction of "binary digit;" the basic unit for storing information. A bit is either a 0 or a 1, which correspond, respectively, to a switch being off or on.

bit-mapped graphic An image that is saved ("mapped") in computer memory as a pattern of bits; each pixel (dot of light) on the display screen is represented by its own bit(s). One bit per pixel enables a user to create black-and-white images, two bits per pixel provides the user with four colors, and eight bits per pixel provides 256 colors. *Contrasts with* object-oriented graphic.

bit rate *see* baud rate.

bits per second (bps) A unit of measurement used to describe the speed of data transmission; for example, a modem may send data at 9600 bps; *see* baud rate.

black box A slang term for an electronic device that functions as specified but whose internal mechanism is mysterious to the user; the opposite of a glass box.

block A group of characters, words, or records that can be treated as a single unit during processing or data transmission. For example, in word processing, a user can mark a block of text in a document, then press a button to reset the entire block to a different line width—or press a button to transfer the block to another location in the document.

board *see* printed circuit board.

boilerplate document A letter or other document composed at least in part of standard paragraphs that previously were saved on disk; useful for routine tasks such as providing sales terms, writing wills, preparing contracts, etc.

boot or **boot up** Start a computer or load an application program; from the phrase, "pull yourself up by the bootstraps."

boot disk *see* system disk.

bps *see* bits per second.

branch One of the possible paths, or courses of action, along which a computer program may proceed.

bridge A device used to connect two local area networks (LANs), allowing them to exchange data even though they may have different topologies, communications protocols, etc.; operates at the second level of the Open Systems Interconnection (OSI) model; *contrasts with* router.

browse To search through information; often used to describe looking through data in a database or messages on a bulletin board.

bubble memory   A memory device that stores information by means of microscopic magnetic domains ("bubbles"); the absence or presence of a domain is the basis for a binary 1 or 0.

buffer   A space in memory where data are temporarily held; usually refers to a space where data are held during transfer between two devices that operate at different speeds, such as a computer (faster) and a printer (slower).

bug   An error in hardware or software that prevents it from running correctly. The original bug was a moth that short-circuited a connection in an early computer.

built-in font   A font that is built into a printer's read-only memory (ROM); also called resident font; *contrasts with* cartridge font.

bulletin board system (BBS)   A public, on-line bulletin board that allows callers to read messages left by other callers, leave their own messages, converse or play games with other callers, download programs for use on their computers, etc.

bundled software   Software that is packaged and sold with a computer.

bus   An electrical path that links components of a computer system.

bus topology   A local area network (LAN) layout that links workstations to a single cable, called a bus; all messages flow over that single cable. Like a party-line telephone, it does not allow two workstations to transmit data at the same time.

byte   The basic unit of computer information, corresponding to one letter, number, punctuation mark, or other symbol. A byte typically consists of a string of eight bits.

C

C   A high-level programming language widely used on the UNIX operating system.

cable   A group of electrical wires sheathed in a protective covering; used to connect two pieces of hardware, such as a computer and a printer.

cache   A small, very fast buffer located between the microprocessor and the main memory; used to speed access to often-used commands and data.

CAD   *see* computer-aided design.

CAD/CAM   *see* computer-aided design and manufacturing.

CAE   *see* computer-aided engineering.

CAI   *see* computer-aided instruction.

callback modem   A modem used for security purposes. When called, but before transmission of data can begin, the modem calls back a preprogrammed number associated with the sending modem. Both sender and receiver need special equipment.

cancel   (1) To stop a program command from running; usually activated by pressing the Esc key. (2) In word processing, to undo a deletion command and recover deleted text.

card   A kind of expansion (printed-circuit) board that plugs into an expansion slot and gives the computer extra capability, such as more memory or a better-quality display.

cartridge font   A font contained in a cartridge that plugs into the printer; used by certain laser and dot-matrix printers; *contrasts with* built-in font.

cascade   In a windowing environment, an arrangement of windows on a display screen so that they overlap one another, with the title bar of each window remaining visible.

CASE   *see* computer-aided software engineering.

cathode ray tube (CRT)   The display technology, or "picture tube," used in desktop computer monitors and television sets; the term often is used as a synonym for "monitor."

CCITT *see* Comité Consultatif International Téléphonique et Télégraphique.

CD-ROM An acronym for Compact Disk — Read-Only Memory; a nonmagnetic storage medium that stores read-only memory on disks that are written on and read by lasers; you can read the data but you cannot change it or add to it.

cell A specific location in a spreadsheet, at the intersection of a row and a column. A cell's address is identified by its coordinates—the letter that labels the column and the number that labels the row.

central processing unit (CPU) The central processor of a computer system. It interprets software instructions, executes arithmetic and logical operations, and maintains control over the system's hardware.

CGA see VGA.

character A letter, number, or symbol such as a punctuation mark that can be stored and processed by a computer. Each character is represented within the computer by an 8-bit (1 byte) binary number.

character recognition A technology used to sense — and encode into machine language — written or printed characters that can be read by people. For example, banks use magnetic ink character recognition (MICR) to encode numbers on bank checks; publishing companies use optical character recognition (OCR) to encode typewritten text.

character set The set of characters that is handled by a specific device or system; usually includes letters, numbers, a blank, special characters ($, %, [,], etc.), and operation characters (+, −, *, =, etc.).

characters per inch (cpi) A unit of measurement that indicates the number of characters that will print in one linear inch. For example, elite, a common typewriter and computer printer type, provides 12 cpi.

characters per second (cps) A unit of measurement used to describe the speed of a printer or communications device.

chat To have a conversation with someone through a bulletin board system.

chip A small, thin silicon wafer (about the size of a fingernail) on which is etched an integrated circuit. Chips are the building blocks of a computer.

CIM *see* computer-integrated manufacturing.

circuit The path along which an electric current flows.

circuit board *see* printed circuit board.

circuit breaker A device that automatically opens ("breaks") an electric circuit in the case of excessive current or other abnormal conditions.

clear To erase, such as the contents of a storage device or the image on a display screen.

click To press and release the mouse button (typically when the mouse pointer is positioned over an object, such as an icon, on the display screen).

clip art Images stored on disk and ready to be electronically "clipped out" and "pasted into" a document. Commercial collections of clip art are widely used in preparing newsletters, business graphics, etc.

clock An electronic circuit within a computer used to synchronize the computer's operations. It generates a series of evenly spaced pulses, called clock pulses. The frequency at which the pulses are emitted is called the clock rate. The higher the clock rate, the greater the number of operations per second that the computer is able to perform.

clone A computer that is compatible with a more expensive brand-name computer; it operates in a similar manner and can accept and process programs written for the brand-name computer.

The term usually refers to a computer that is compatible with an IBM PC.

CMI *see* computer-managed instruction.

coaxial cable A type of transmission medium widely used to connect hardware in local area networks (LANs); more expensive but faster than twisted-pair cable. The cable contains two wires, one surrounding the other.

COBOL An acronym for COmmon Business Oriented Language; a high-level programming language that is widely used in business.

code The set of instructions that makes up a computer program.

coding The process of writing a computer program.

COGO An acronym for COordinated GeOmetry; a high-level programming language used in civil engineering.

cold boot To start the computer by turning on the switch; *contrasts with* warm boot.

column In a spreadsheet, a vertical series of cells, typically identified by letters of the alphabet across the top of the sheet; *contrasts with* row.

Comité Consultatif International Téléphonique et Télégraphique (CCITT) A committee established by the world's telecommunications authorities that sets international communications standards; its two main series of standards are the V series, for communications over public telephone networks, and the X series, for communications over special-purpose data networks.

command An instruction to a program that tells it what to do. For example, a "save" command causes the contents of a file to be saved onto a disk; a "print" command causes the contents of a file to be printed.

command-driven program A program that requires users to memorize keyboard commands for choosing program options; *contrasts with* menu-driven program.

common carrier An organization (either public or private, depending on the country) that provides telephone and other telecommunications services to the public.

communications protocols Standards for the transfer of data among computers via public telephones.

communications server *see* gateway computer.

communications software An application program that enables a computer, modem, and telephone to work together so that data can be sent to and received from distant computers.

compatible (1) The ability of a piece of hardware to work with another piece of hardware. (2) The ability of a computer to accept and process programs and data prepared for another computer.

compile The process of translating a program written in a high-level language into machine language; this is done using a compiler.

compiler A computer program used by programmers to translate programs written in a high-level language (such as BASIC or COBOL) into machine language, which can be understood by the computer's central processing unit (CPU). The resulting machine code is saved as a program file ready to be run at any time.

component (1) A basic part of a computer system, such as a printer, disk drive, or keyboard. (2) A basic part of an electric circuit, such as a transistor or diode.

compressed type *see* condensed type.

computer A programmable electronic device that can perform calculations and process information.

computer-aided design (CAD) The use of a computer system to assist in the design of a wide range of products, from electronic circuits and machine parts to furniture and automobiles.

computer-aided design and manufacturing (CAD/CAM) The use of computers in the design and creation of a product, including the automation of a broad range of manufacturing tasks.

computer-aided engineering (CAE) The use of interactive computer graphics and other software to solve engineering problems (stress analysis, fluid flow, etc.) and to design objects (bridges, airplane landing gears, etc.).

computer-aided instruction (CAI) The use of a computer system as a learning tool. CAI software includes tutorials, drill-and-practice programs, simulations, etc.

computer-aided software engineering (CASE) The automation of the software engineering process. Development of new software is speeded through the use of computer-based charting and diagramming tools, code generators, error checkers, compilers, etc.

computer crime A broad term for any crime involving computers, such as unauthorized modifications to or destruction of data, stealing data or money, piracy of copyright-protected software, and breaking into or sabotaging systems.

computer engineer A person who designs and develops computer equipment.

computer fraud The illegal manipulation of data within a computer system for financial gain or other purposes; for example, embezzling money from a customer account or changing information in a student's grade file.

computer graphics The use of a computer system to generate and process charts, drawings, and other visual information (as opposed to text information).

computer-integrated manufacturing (CIM) The use of CAD/CAM and other software in all steps of the manufacturing process, including design, scheduling, production, inventory control, and marketing.

computer literate Understanding computers, their functions, and how to use them.

computer-managed instruction (CMI) The use of computers in schools to manage administrative and clerical tasks, such as producing tests and lesson plans, computing grades, and keeping track of attendance.

computerphobia Anxiety marked by a fear of computers.

computer science The study of computers, including such topics as architecture, systems analysis, hardware design, programming theory, artificial intelligence, and applications.

computer system Hardware, including at least one computer, that is interconnected and designed to work together. A typical home or office system might include a computer, a monitor, a printer, and both hard and floppy disk drives.

condensed type Printer type in which the characters are not as wide as standard characters; useful for such tasks as fitting wide tables or spreadsheets onto a sheet of paper; *also called* compressed type.

configuration All the components of a computer system (terminals, disk drives, modems, etc.) and how they are connected to one another.

connect time The time actually spent connected to a bulletin board or other on-line service.

continuous-form paper Paper fed into a printer on a continuous roll; usable on tractor-feed printers. The paper is perforated at intervals so that it can be easily separated into standard-sized sheets after printing; *also called* fanfold paper.

continuous processing A method of processing data in which data are processed immediately, rather than being stored to be processed in batches; *also called* on-line processing, real-time processing, and transaction processing.

control bus An electrical path used to send timing signals and other control signals from one chip to another.

control code In ASCII, 32 codes (from 0 to 31) that perform hardware-control functions; for example, a printer may use one control code to start *italic* text and another to turn it off.

CONTROL key A key on the keyboard of some computer systems that, when pressed simultaneously with one or more additional keys, performs a program command. For example, in some word processing programs, pressing Ctrl and A moves the cursor left one word.

controller A circuit that controls the operation of a device attached to the computer; for example, a disk drive controller controls disk drives.

control unit The part of the central processing unit (CPU) that coordinates all computer operations, including the sequence in which program instructions are executed.

coprocessor A special chip, or microprocessor, added to a computer to speed the execution of mathematical, graphics, or some other specific type of computation.

copy To transfer data from one location to another, such as from the computer's internal memory to a disk.

copy protection Any of various techniques used to make it theoretically impossible to copy the contents of a disk, thereby protecting software on the disk against unauthorized duplication.

cpi *see* characters per inch.

CP/M An acronym for Control Program for Microprocessors; an operating system widely used for 8-bit computers (computers that process one byte—8 bits—of information at a time); replaced by MS-DOS as the industry standard after the IBM PC was introduced.

cps *see* characters per second.

CPU *see* central processing unit.

crash To suddenly stop working; a malfunction in a piece of hardware or a serious error in a program can cause a crash.

cross talk In communications, signals that leak, or "cross," from one cable to another, causing errors on the second cable; usually occurs because the cables are too close to one another.

CRT *see* cathode ray tube.

current drive *see* default drive.

cursor A small, movable spot of light on the display screen that indicates where data are to be entered or erased.

cursor control keys Keys on a computer keyboard marked with arrows and used to control the movement of the cursor. The direction of the arrow indicates in which direction that key moves the cursor.

customer support Assistance given to the buyer of a piece of hardware or software, either by the manufacturer or the vendor. For example, customer support for a database package might include a 30-day warranty, a toll-free number to call for assistance in using the package, and a quarterly newsletter containing tips on how to expand applications of the package.

cut and paste In word processing and some other applications, to remove text from a document (cut) and put it (paste) elsewhere in the same document or in another document.

cut sheet feeder *see* sheet feeder.

D

daisy-wheel printer A letter-quality impact printer that has a circular printing element composed of a series of spokes, or "petals," each of which contains molded characters; the printing element rotates until the desired character is in position to be struck by a hammer.

data Information (*singular*: datum).

databank *see* information service.

database An organized collection of data; for example, a mailing list, patient records, or baseball statistics.

database-management system (DBMS) An application program designed to store, retrieve, and keep track of information in a database.

data bus An electrical path that carries information (data) — for example, between the central processing unit (CPU) and memory.

data collision In a local area network (LAN), when two work-stations send data simultaneously along the same pathway.

data communications The transfer of information from one place to another using computers.

data link In spreadsheets and other application programs, a connection between two files or data items that causes a change in one file to also be made in the second file. For example, a work-sheet listing monthly sales figures can be linked to a worksheet listing annual totals.

data processing The use of computers to sort, add, rearrange, and otherwise manipulate information.

data recovery program A program designed to "undo" file dele-tion or the formatting of a disk.

data validation A feature of some application programs where-by the computer confirms that the right basic type of informa-tion has been entered. For example, a database program will not allow a user to enter a name in a space reserved for a phone number.

DBMS *see* database-management system.

debug To locate and correct errors ("bugs") in a computer pro-gram.

debugger A program that helps a programmer locate and correct errors ("bugs") in a program.

decode To translate binary code into an understandable form; *contrasts with* encode.

dedicated A device designed or used for a specific purpose; for example, a dedicated file server is a computer used exclusively for running a network.

default A predefined response by a computer system to a command; the computer chooses this response unless the user specifies otherwise. For example, in a word processing program, a document may automatically be printed 50 lines to a page; this default setting can be countermanded for a single document or changed to a new setting.

default drive The disk drive on which the computer stores and from which it retrieves files, unless you instruct otherwise; *also called* the active drive or current drive.

delete To remove, or erase; for example, to erase a record from a file or a file from a disk.

demultiplexer In communications, a linking device that can route a message from one line into many separate lines.

density A measure of the amount of data that can be stored on a magnetic storage device. For example, a double-density floppy disk can hold 720 kilobytes.

desk manager A memory-resident program that provides the user with instant access to a variety of tools, such as a calculator, notepad, appointment calendar, address book, and phone dialer.

desktop computer A microcomputer that is small enough to sit on the top of a desk. Before the age of laptop and notebook computers, "desktop" was synonymous with "personal computer."

desktop organizer *see* desk manager.

desktop publishing The production of high-quality newsletters, brochures, and other printed matter using a personal computer and a printer.

destination file The file on a disk that receives data following a "save" command; *contrasts with* source file.

device driver A program, usually installed with the operating system, that lets the computer recognize and communicate with an external device, such as a printer or monitor.

diagnostic program A progam used to determine if hardware or software is functioning properly and if not, to locate the source of the problem. Some computers have built-in diagnostic programs.

digital Composed of, or employing, discrete, binary representations of information; *contrasts with* analog.

digital computer A computer that accepts, performs computations on, and represents data in digital form, as discrete numbers composed of binary digits (1s and 0s).

digitize To put data in digital form; for example, to convert a photograph into a series of bits.

DIP (Dual In-line Package) switch An on-off switch mounted on a circuit board that can be changed by the user to choose operating characteristics of peripherals; for example, a certain printer DIP switch may set a page length of 12 inches when it is in the "on" position and a page length of 11 inches in the "off" position.

direction keys The four arrow keys on a computer keyboard, named for the direction the arrow points: UP ARROW, DOWN ARROW, LEFT ARROW, and RIGHT ARROW.

directory A list of the files stored on a disk. In some operating systems, including MS-DOS, the DIR ("directory") command displays the directory on the screen.

directory tree A graphic representation of the files stored on a disk; resembles the branching structure of an upside-down tree. The top-level directory, called the root directory, branches into a number of subdirectories, which may branch into even smaller subdirectories.

disassembler A program that translates machine language into assembly language.

disk A flat, circular platter with a magnetic surface on which data can be stored; the two main types are floppy disks and hard disks.

disk alignment notches Two small, semicircular notches on the forward end of the jacket of a 5.25-inch floppy disk; used to ensure that the disk is properly aligned inside the disk drive.

disk directory *see* directory.

disk drive A storage device designed to read information from and write information on disks.

disk drive controller *see* controller.

diskette *synonymous with* floppy disk.

disk server A hard disk drive that "serves" the needs of all the workstations on a local area network (LAN). It has special software that partitions the disk into separate volumes for different users.

display The visual representation of data on the screen of a monitor.

document Anything created with an application program that can be given a name and saved as a file; for example, a memo, mailing list, or graph.

documentation The printed instructions that explain how to use a computer program.

DOS An acronym for Disk Operating System and shorthand for MS-DOS, the standard operating system for 16-bit (and most 32-bit) IBM and IBM-compatible personal computers.

DOS prompt In MS-DOS, the letter designation for the active (default) disk drive; appears at the left side of the display screen and is followed by a colon.

DOS shell A utility program designed to make it easier for users to interface with MS-DOS. For example, the shell may allow a person to use menus to handle common operations such as changing directories, rather than having to memorize the MS-DOS commands for such operations.

dot matrix printer An impact printer that forms a character from a matrix pattern of tiny dots. Each dot is made by a pin stiking an inked ribbon and pushing it against the paper.

dots per inch (dpi) A unit of measurement for the resolution of display screens, printers, and scanners; indicates the number of dots the device can produce in a line one inch long; for example, a 600 dpi laser printer.

double-click To rapidly press and release the mouse button twice without moving the mouse; often used to select and open a file.

double-density disk A floppy disk that can store twice as much data per unit area as now-obsolete single-density disks.

double-sided disk A floppy disk that uses both sides for data storage, thereby having double the storage capacity of now-obsolete single-sided disks.

down A slang term for "not in operation." A computer is down when it is turned off, receiving scheduled or unscheduled maintenance, or not functioning.

download To receive a program, file, or other data from another computer via a modem. For example, a person may download a file from a bulletin board for use on his or her own computer; *contrasts with* upload.

downtime A period of time during which a computer or other device is not working, either because of machine failure or because it is being serviced for regular maintenance.

downward compatible Able to work, without modifications, with older hardware models or software versions. For example, Intel's 32-bit 80386 microprocessor can run programs designed for Intel's earlier 16-bit 80286 microprocessor.

dpi *see* dots per inch.

draft quality A printer quality available on dot-matrix printers. Because draft uses a minimum number of dots per character, it produces a high speed but low-resolution printout; *compare with* near-letter quality.

drag After placing the mouse pointer on an object, holding down the mouse button, moving the mouse, and then releasing the button; generally used to choose a menu item or to move an object on the display screen.

DRAM An acronym for Dynamic Random Access Memory; *also called* dynamic RAM; a semiconductor memory chip that stores information on a very short-term basis. The chip must be constantly recharged or the data will be lost.

draw program A graphics program that stores each image as a discrete object, such as a letter, line, square or circle. Draw programs are particularly useful for making diagrams. CAD programs are examples of draw programs; *contrasts with* paint program.

drill-and-practice programs Educational software designed to help students review material already learned and to reinforce skills; for example, programs that provide practice in shape recognition, arithmetic, and typing.

drive *see* disk drive.

drive name Floppy disk drives usually are referred to as the A drive and B drive (assuming the computer has two such drives); the hard disk drive usually is referred to as the C drive. A drive name consists of the drive letter followed by a colon. For example, if the default drive is drive C and the user wishes to access a file called TENNIS on drive A, he or she must type the drive name before the file name — A:TENNIS

driver *see* device driver.

dumb terminal A terminal consisting of a keyboard and a monitor, and connected to a central computer in a multiuser system. It can send and receive data but, because it lacks a central processing unit (CPU) and disk drives, it cannot process data; *contrasts with* smart terminal.

dump (1) To transfer the contents of a computer's main memory to a printer or an external storage device. (2) To list the contents of all or part of a computer's main memory; often done by programmers during debugging.

duplicate To reproduce without changing the original. For example, a duplicate disk contains copies of all the files stored on an original (master) disk.

dynamic RAM *see* DRAM.

E

EBCDIC *see* extended binary coded decimal interchange code.

EDI *see* electronic data exchange.

edit To change data; for example, deleting a sentence from a letter, redrawing a chart, or inserting mortgage payments into a spreadsheet.

EFTS *see* Electronic Funds Transfer Systems.

EGA *see* VGA.

electromagnetic radiation *see* VDT radiation.

electronic data exchange (EDI) (1) The exchange of standard documents, such as invoices and purchase orders, between computer systems. (2) The standards that specify the structure and format of documents to be exchanged between computer systems.

Electronic Funds Transfer Systems (EFTS) Systems that electronically transfer money between financial institutions and between these institutions and the accounts of their customers.

electronic mail Letters, memos, and other written messages sent from one computer to another, either over telephone lines or over a local area network; often called E-mail.

electronic stylus A penlike device that can be used to write, draw, and make program choices directly on the display screen.

electronic thesaurus A program (often part of a word processing package) that provides synonyms for words; comparable to a thesaurus in print form.

E-mail *see* electronic mail.

embedded computer A computer installed in another machine and programmed to make the machine work more efficiently. Telephones, VCRs, robots, automobiles, and airplanes are among the thousands of products that have embedded computers.

emulate To imitate the way another computer device or system works. For example, a less-expensive printer may emulate a brand-name printer. The hardware within a device that permits it to emulate another device is called the emulator.

encode To translate data into binary code; *contrasts with* decode.

encryption The coding of sensitive data prior to storage or transmission to prevent unauthorized access; an effective computer security technique.

end user The person who actually uses a computer or a program, as opposed to the manufacturers and sellers of such products.

ENTER key A key on the keyboard that is used for different purposes by various application programs; for example, in word processing, hitting the ENTER key starts a new paragraph; called the RETURN key on some computers, such as the Macintosh.

entry An item of data in a list, table, etc.

EPROM *see* erasable programmable read-only memory.

erasable programmable read-only memory (EPROM) A type of internal-memory chip that can be reprogrammed several hundred times.

erase To remove, or delete; for example, to erase a record from a file or a file from a disk.

error detection and correction In telecommunications software, program routines that detect and correct errors (such as those caused by static on telephone lines) during data transfer.

error message A message displayed on the screen to inform the user that the program cannot continue. The message indicates the nature of the problem (error), so the user can determine how to correct it. For example, the MS-DOS message "bad command or file name" indicates that MS-DOS cannot find the program the user asked it to run.

execute To carry out the instructions of a computer program.

expandable The ability to add more memory, disk drives, and other capabilities to a computer. Knowing a computer's expandability is important when purchasing a machine.

expanded memory Memory above 640K on an IBM PC or PC-compatible computer. Taking advantage of expanded memory under MS-DOS requires an expanded memory board or special software.

expansion board A printed circuit board that plugs into a slot in the computer and provides added capabilities, such as additional ports, memory, or functions.

expansion slot A slot in a computer into which an expansion board can be installed.

expert system A computer program that uses artificial intelligence techniques, such as rules of inference, plus an extensive database, to simulate the decision-making ability of human experts.

export To send data from one program or location to another; for example, exporting a customer address list from a customer database to a label printing program.

Extended Binary Coded Decimal Interchange Code (EBCDIC) A computer code used in IBM mainframes; each character is represented by an 8-bit binary number. The acronym is pronounced "ebb-see-dick."

extension The second, optional part of a file name, consisting of a period followed by up to three letters; used to identify the kind of information the file contains; for example, text files normally have the extension .TXT.

external drive A hard disk drive that has its own case, cables, and power supply; *contrasts with* internal drive.

external memory Memory stored on magnetic disks or tapes; *contrasts with* primary memory, which resides within the central processing unit (CPU); *also called* secondary storage.

external modem A modem that has its own case and is connected by cable to the computer's serial interface; unlike an internal modem, can easily be used by any computer.

F

fanfold paper *see* continuous-form paper.

FAT *see* File Allocation Table.

FAX card An expansion board that plugs into a computer and gives it the ability to send and receive documents via telecommunications. The card sends files created in the computer and turns documents received from other FAX machines into computer files.

FDDI An acronym for Fiber Distributed Data Interface; a standard for connecting devices and networks using fiber optic cables, with data transmission in excess of 100 megabits per second.

feedback (1) In interactive software, the program's response to input from the user. (2) The use of part of the output of a machine or process as input into the same machine or process at a later stage, to control, evaluate, or correct performance.

feed holes The holes along the sides of continuous-form printer paper; sprockets on the printer engage in these holes to pull the paper through the printer.

female connector In computer cabling, a connection device that has sockets designed to accept the pins of a male connector.

fiber optic cable A type of transmission medium increasingly used in networks and other communications systems. The cable has a central core of many thin, glass fibers, each surrounded by a sheath (cladding) to avoid interference between fibers.

fiber optics A transmission technology that uses light pulses rather than variations in electrical current to relay data; the light pulses travel through flexible glass fibers no thicker than a human hair; offers many advantages over traditional copper cable, including less weight and bulk, greater transmission capacity, and immunity to electrical interference.

field In a database, the smallest unit of information. For example, a customer record is likely to include a name field, a street address field, a city field, a state field, a zip code field, and a telephone number field.

field engineer A person who repairs computer equipment; generally employed by a equipment manufacturer, vendor, or computer repair service.

FIFO *see* first-in first-out.

file (1) A unit of information stored in the computer's memory or on a disk or tape and identified by a file name. (2) In a database, a group of related records; for example, a mailing list, a payroll file, or a telephone directory.

File Allocation Table (FAT) A record on a floppy disk or hard disk that keeps track of the location of each file stored on the disk; also allocates free space on the disk. FAT is transparent, or invisible, to the user.

file extension *see* extension.

file link *see* data link.

file locking A networking procedure that prevents two or more users from simultaneously accessing the same file; *see* also record locking.

file management program   A database program that organizes data into a single file, such as a mailing list, supplier list, or student test-grades list; *also called* a file manager.

file name   A name used to identify a file on a disk.

file server   A computer in a local area network (LAN), usually equipped with a large hard disk or other storage facility, that maintains application programs and common databases, and handles network administration; *also called* a network server. A dedicated file server is used solely for these purposes. Some LANs use distributed file servers—several computers that share ("distribute") processing activities.

firmware   A slang term for programs that are permanently stored ("firm") in a computer's read-only memory (ROM) and cannot be changed or erased except under certain conditions.

first-in first out (FIFO)   A type of memory buffer used to accommodate varying data transfer rates by elements of a computer system.

flame or **flame mail**   In bulletin board systems, a message that disagrees violently with another user's point of view, often in derogatory or obscene language. A series of flames exchanged by two or more users is called a mail war.

flat-panel display   The type of display found on laptops and other small portable computers; instead of a cathode-ray tube, it generally uses liquid crystal technology.

FLIPS   An acronym for Fuzzy Logic Inferences Per Second; a measurement of the speed of operation of a fuzzy logic computer chip.

floating point arithmetic   A method of calculating numbers in which the position of the decimal point is not fixed, but "floats"; each number is represented by a fixed part and an exponent—for example, 6.7924×10^3; used for processing very large numbers and to improve the accuracy of calculations.

floppy disk   A thin flexible disk made of plastic and encased in a protective jacket; used for external memory storage. The disk is coated with a magnetic material on which data can be recorded. "Floppies" come in 5.25- and 3.5-inch sizes.

FLOPS An acronym for Floating Point Operations Per Second; a measurement of the speed of computation in the central processing unit (CPU).

flowchart A graphic outline of the logic of a computer program, used as an aid in programming and composed of various symbols that represent different types of operations. For example, a parallelogram represents an input or output statement; a diamond represents a decision.

flow control *see* handshake.

flush In word processing, the alignment of text along a margin. Text may be only flush left, with a ragged right-hand margin; only flush right; or flush left and right.

font A collection of characters (letters, numbers, punctuation marks, and symbols) with the same typeface (design) and size (measured in points); for example, 8-point Times or 10-point Helvetica.

font cartridge A cartridge that is plugged into a printer to supply one or more fonts (in addition to the fonts built into the printer's memory).

font size *see* type size.

footer In a document created with a word processing program, a line of text, such as a chapter title, printed at the bottom of a page. Special commands are used to create footers and to indicate on which pages they should appear (all pages, right-hand pages only, etc.); *contrasts with* header.

footprint The space that a computer or other device takes up on a desk. Some machines have bigger footprints than others.

forecasting Using a spreadsheet to make financial predictions based on "what-if" questions: for example, *what* would happen to a family's monthly mortgage payments *if* they switched from a 30-year mortgage at 9.5% to a 15-year mortgage at 8.75%?

format (1) To prepare a disk for use by partitioning it into a pattern of magnetic sectors and tracks; *also called* initializing the disk. (2) In word processing and some other application programs, to specify how text and other data is to appear on the printed page.

form feed A command issued by a program to a printer using continuous-form paper, telling it to advance the paper to the top of the next page.

FORTH A high-level language programming language used in astronomy, robotics, and other applications; from "FOuRTH generation language."

FORTRAN An acronym for FORmula TRANslation; a high-level programming language often used for scientific and engineering applications.

freeware *see* public-domain software.

friction feed A friction-based mechanism that enables a printer to advance ("feed in") one sheet of paper at a time; *contrasts with* tractor feed.

full duplex In asynchronous communications, a transmission link that is able to send and receive information at the same time; *contrasts with* half duplex.

function keys Keys on some computer keyboards that are labelled F1, F2, etc. Programs can assign specific commands to these keys, such as "save this file" or "count the number of words in this file." Pressing a function key, perhaps in combination with other keys, initiates execution of an assigned command.

fuzzy logic system A computer system that can work with imprecise terms, such as "cold" or "slightly." Researchers in fuzzy logic believe the technology can have important applications in such areas as artificial intelligence and controlling industrial processes.

G

garbage Faulty data, meaningless characters, incorrect computer commands, or any other undesirable characters that appear on the screen; an indication that something is wrong in the system.

garbage in, garbage out (GIGO) A slang term indicating that if a user enters unreliable or useless data into a program (garbage in), the program will produce unreliable or useless results (garbage out).

gas plasma screen A type of screen used on some laptops; the display is produced by applying an electric current to an ionized gas contained behind a transparent panel.

gateway computer A computer (plus related software) used to link a local area network (LAN) with other networks, including wide-area networks (WANs), and with mainframe computers; *also called* a communications server.

general-purpose computer A computer designed to handle a wide variety of applications; *contrasts with* special-purpose computer.

general-purpose language A high-level programming language that can be used on many different types of computers for many different purposes (applications); examples include BASIC, COBOL, and FORTRAN.

ghost A permanent image etched into the display screen, formed when the image is left on the screen for an extended period of time; *also called* phosphor burn-in. Ghosts can be prevented by using a screen saver program or by turning down the brightness of the display when the computer is not being used.

gigabyte (G, GB) A unit of measurement for computer memory; equals approximately 1 billion bytes or characters (specifically, 1,024 megabytes).

giga instructions per seconds (gips) A measurement used to describe the speed at which a central processing unit (CPU) can process instructions; one gips equals one billion instructions per second.

GIGO *see* garbage in, garbage out.

gips *see* giga instructions per second.

glare Harsh, uncomfortable light coming from the display screen; can cause eyestrain; can be reduced by good lighting and by placing an antiglare filter over the screen.

glitch A hardware malfunction caused by a sudden voltage surge or electrical noise.

global search In word processing, to use a single command to locate all occurrences of a word or phrase in a document. The user then has the option of changing these on an individual basis or using a command to do a global replace — that is, replace the word or phrase everywhere it occurs with a different word or phrase.

grammar checker A program (often part of a word processing package) that scans a document and locates common grammatical errors, such as subject/verb disagreement, redundant phrases, overly long sentences, incomplete sentences, etc.; *also called* a style checker.

graphic user interface (GUI) A program that allows a person to interact with a computer by pointing to graphic symbols on the display screen (generally, using a mouse) rather than typing in instructions. The four main elements of a GUI are windows, icons, mice, and pull-down menus.

graphics Pictorial displays such as charts, graphs, drawings, etc.; *contrasts with* text.

graphics adapter card A circuit board, placed either in an expansion slot or directly on the motherboard, that enables the computer to display graphics.

graphics editor A program that can change (edit) images that already exist in computer-readable form.

graphics tablet An input device that transforms images drawn on its flat surface into images displayed on the display screen.

greeking In desktop publishing, converting text into lines or bars ("greek") so that a simulated version of an entire page can be displayed on the screen, allowing the user to view and assess the page's layout.

grid In optical character recognition, two sets of lines used to specify or measure characters.

groupware Software and other products that help groups of workers do their jobs better — by, for example, controlling workflow, helping workers communicate and share information, or allowing workers to annotate documents without altering the original documents.

GUI *see* graphic user interface.

H

hacker (1) A computer enthusiast—usually an amateur—who takes much enjoyment in programming, finding bugs, solving problems with computers, etc. (2) Someone who tries to gain unauthorized access to a computer system.

half duplex In asynchronous communications, a transmission link that is able to send and receive information, but not at the same time; *contrasts with* full duplex.

handshake A flow-control signal sent by one computer to another in order to establish a connection and agree on protocols for data transmission.

hard copy A printout on paper of a document, graph, or other computer data; *contrasts with* soft copy.

hard disk A rigid disk with a metallic recording surface, encased in a sealed cartridge; used for external memory storage; *also called* a fixed disk.

hard disk drive A storage device, usually built into the computer, for external memory storage; consists of a sealed cartridge containing a single magnetically coated disk or a stack of several disks; holds much more memory than a floppy disk.

hardware The physical components of a computer system, such as integrated circuits, keyboard, printer, and disk drives; *contrasts with* software.

Hayes compatible Used to describe a modem that is compatible with a set of standard commands established by Hayes Microcomputer Products, a leading maker of modems.

head The part of a floppy or hard disk drive that reads data from a disk or writes data onto the disk; *also called* the read/write head.

header In a document created with a word processing program, a line of text, such as a chapter's title, printed at the top of a page. Special commands are used to create headers and to indicate on which pages they should appear (every page, left-hand pages only, etc.); *contrasts with* footer.

help screen In many programs, an easily accessed display of information about the program and how to use it (for example, a summary of which function key does what); generally accessed via a status line or a menu.

hertz (Hz) A measurement of the frequency of an audible tone or alternating electric current, equal to one cycle per second; *see* also megahertz.

heuristic Using trial and error to solve a problem; *contrasts with* an algorithmic approach.

hidden file A file that isn't listed in a normal directory command; system files, such as BIOS files, are examples.

hierarchical database A database in which information is organized like an upside-down tree, with parent files and children files; to access specific information, a user must understand where and how data are sorted; used for many mainframe databases.

high-density disk A floppy disk that can store 1 megabyte or more of data; *synonymous with* quad-density disk.

high-level language A programming language that uses instructions and expressions that are similar to human language; examples include BASIC, COBOL, and FORTRAN; *contrasts with* low-level language (assembly language).

highlight To draw attention to something by making it stand out from its background. For example, a spell checker may highlight a word that is not on its spelling list by making the word appear brighter than other words in the document.

highway Another name for a bus.

home computer A microcomputer that is inexpensive, easy to set up, and easy to use, with sufficient power to handle activities typically performed in a home, such as writing letters, balancing checkbooks, maintaining family medical files, practicing math skills, and playing games.

horizontal display The width, in inches or centimeters, of the display screen.

host computer A computer that provides services which other computers can access via a network. For example, in a wide area network (WAN), the host computer may provide people at work-stations with databases and electronic mail.

Hypercard A powerful data management tool for Macintosh computers that permits users to build, store, and connect in various ways small databases, or stacks, of text, graphics, sound, and animation; programs designed to run under Hypercard are nicknamed "stackware."

hypertext Documents presented in an interactive computer environment; a technique used in multimedia that allows a user to branch from what he or she reads to other text, graphics, or video.

hyphenate To insert a hyphen in the word at the end of a line, thereby making the line break properly at the right margin. Many word processing programs can perform automatic hyphenation, using either a hyphenation dictionary or grammatical rules.

Hz *see* hertz.

I

IC *see* integrated circuit.

icon A graphic symbol on the display screen that represents a file, peripheral, or some other object or function; for example, scissors are generally used to indicate cut-and-paste editing.

illegal character A character that cannot be used in a particular circumstance. For example, in MS-DOS asterisks and commas are illegal characters for file names.

image processing The use of a computer to enhance, restore, analyze, alter, and in other ways process images.

impact printer A printer that forms an image in the same manner as an ordinary typewriter: the printing head strikes an inked ribbon, causing ink to be transferred onto paper. Dot-matrix printers are examples of impact printers.

import To bring in data from another program or location; for example, importing names and addresses from a customer database into a label printing program.

infection The presence of an illegal piece of software, called a virus, within a computer system.

information service A broad-based, on-line collection of databases that can be accessed by the public for a fee. A typical information service offers data such as stock quotes, airline schedules, restaurant guides, and news reports, as well as services such as electronic mail, computer shopping, teleconferencing, and home banking; *also called* a databank or an information utility.

initialize (1) To reset a computer or program to some starting values. (2) To format a disk.

ink-jet printer A non-impact printer that forms an image by spraying ink from tiny nozzles directly onto paper.

input Information entered into a computer (or, when used as a verb, the process of entering information into a computer).

input device A peripheral used to enter information into a computer; examples include keyboards, mice, and scanners.

input/output (I/O) The transfer of data and program instructions between the central processing unit (CPU) and other parts of the computer system. The I/O system (the bus and other components that carry the data and instructions) is an important part of a system's architecture.

install (1) To set up hardware so that it is ready to be used. (2) To put a program on a hard disk.

integrated circuit (IC) An interconnected array of transistors and other electronic components on a single semiconductor chip.

Integrated Services Digital Network (ISDN) A high-speed digital network that can carry both voice and data traffic on the same telephone lines.

integrated software A software package that contains two or more functions, such as word processing and a spreadsheet, has a consistent user interface for all functions, and permits the transfer of data among functions.

interactive software Programs that carry out a dialogue with the user; games are interactive, as is much educational software.

interface *see* port, user interface.

internal drive A hard disk drive that is installed within the computer; *contrasts with* external drive.

internal modem A modem on a printed circuit card that plugs directly into an expansion slot in the computer; requires less space and costs less than an external modem, but also is less versatile.

internal storage *see* primary storage.

International Standards Organization (ISO) An international group composed of standards organization representatives from member nations; the U.S. affiliate is the American National Standards Institute (ANSI). ISO, together with the Institute of

Electrical and Electronic Engineers (IEEE), developed the Open Systems Interconnection (OSI) standards for local area networks (LANs).

interpreter A program that translates instructions written in a high-level language into a low-level language that the computer can understand. An interpreter translates a program step-by-step each time the program is run; *contrasts with* assembler, compiler.

I/O *see* input/output.

ISDN *see* Integrated Services Digital Network.

ISO *see* International Standards Organization.

J

jam signal A signal sent throughout a local area network (LAN) alerting all workstations that a data collision has occurred in the network.

joystick An input device in which directional pushes on a lever (the joystick) impart specific commands to the computer; widely used for playing computer games.

justification In word processing, the alignment of text along a margin; the margin is straight, as opposed to ragged.

K

K *see* kilobyte.

Kermit In asynchronous communications, a transmission protocol used for sending files between computers; much slower than XModem, YModem, and ZModem (the other major protocols used for file transfers).

kerning In desktop publishing and some other application programs that work with text, the ability to adjust the spacing between letters; especially useful for making words in large font sizes, such as those in headlines, look attractive.

keyboard An input device consisting of an array of keys arranged similarly to the keys of an ordinary typewriter; when a key is pressed, a coded signal is sent to the computer.

keypad A group of keys numbered 0 through 9 and arranged in a rectangle on the far right side of a keyboard; designed for the rapid entry of numerical data. On some keyboards, some of the number keys also function as cursor movement keys; a user moves from one function to the other by pressing the NumLock key located above the keypad.

keystroke The act of pressing down a key on the computer keyboard, thereby entering a character or initiating a command.

kilobyte (K, KB) A unit of measurement for computer memory; equals approximately 1 thousand bytes or characters (specifically, 1,024 bytes).

knowledge base In an expert system, a collection of facts that represent the common knowledge of experts in that particular subject area.

L

LAN *see* local area network.

language *see* programming language.

laptop computer A portable computer that is small and light enough to be operated on a user's lap. It uses a lightweight display, usually a liquid crystal display, and can run off batteries.

large-scale integration (LSI) chip A silicon chip that contains up to 100,000 transistors; *see also* very large scale integration chip.

laser disk *see* optical disk.

laser printer A non-impact printer that uses the same techniques as a photocopy machine and produces a very high-quality printout. A laser forms images of text and other data on a light-sensitive, rotating drum; dry (xerographic) ink is attracted to the images and then transferred to paper.

lasso In a paint program, a feature that allows the user to encircle an irregular area of the picture, then move, copy, or make some other change to the area.

last-in first-out (LIFO) A type of memory buffer used to accommodate varying data transfer rates by elements of a computer system.

layout In publishing, the arrangement of text and graphics on a page. Laying out a page may involve altering the style and size of headlines and body type, resizing line graphics and digitized photos, adding column rules, etc.— all of which can be done quickly with a desktop publishing program.

LCD *see* liquid crystal display.

LED *see* light-emitting diode.

letter quality Type produced by a printer that looks as good as type produced by a high-quality typewriter; daisy-wheel printers are letter-quality printers; *see also* near-letter quality.

license agreement A written agreement provided by a software publisher and enclosed in a software package; it defines a user's rights and obligations and limits the liability of the publisher. Use of the software implies acceptance of the agreement's terms; *see also* site license.

LIFO *see* last-in first-out.

light-emitting diode (LED) A small electronic device that emits light when current flows through it; used for indicator lights on computers, modems, printers, etc.

light pen An input device consisting of a stylus containing a photocell that detects light; can be used to select items from program menus or to draw on a display screen or graphics tablet.

linker A special program that joins together separate programs, enabling them to run as a single program. Many application programs actually consist of a series of programs linked together.

liquid crystal display (LCD) A low-power display technology used in the flat-panel displays of small computers such as laptops and notebooks.

LISP An acronym for LISt Processing; a high-level programming language used in artificial intelligence applications.

list (1) An ordered set of data. (2) To print or otherwise display data.

load The electronic transfer of a program from a storage device, such as a disk, into the computer's random-access memory (RAM), where it can be used.

local area network (LAN) A group of computers and peripherals linked together by high-speed cables and contained within a limited area, such as a building; allows users to communicate with one another, exchange information, and share resources (including peripherals, databases, and programs).

local drive In a local area network (LAN), a disk drive used by one workstation; *contrasts with* network drive.

local printer In a local area network (LAN), a printer used by one workstation; *contrasts with* network printer.

logical operations Operations that define the logical relationships between two quantities or conditions; for example, comparing two numbers to determine which one is bigger or comparing a value against an average to determine if the value is average, above average, or below average.

logic board *see* motherboard.

LOGO A high-level programming language that uses an on-screen pointer called a turtle; often used to teach logical thinking and programming fundamentals to young children.

log off To end a connection with a remote computer system (such as a bulletin board or information utility).

log on To establish a connection with, or gain access to, a remote computer system (such as a bulletin board or information utility).

low-level language A term sometimes used as a synonym for assembly language, because programming instructions written in assembly language are very similar to machine language, even though they are written in symbolic form rather than in 1s and 0s; *contrasts with* high-level language.

LSI *see* large-scale integration chip.

M

machine code A synonym for binary code. A string of machine code might look like is: 1001 1000 0010 0101.

machine language The lowest-level programming language, consisting of strings of binary digits (0s and 1s) that can be read and understood by a computer's central processing unit (CPU). Programmers seldom work in machine language; rather, they write programs in a high-level language or in assembly language, then use a special program (either a compiler, an assembler, or an interpreter) to translate their programs into machine language.

macro A set of instructions stored in a program; the instructions can be executed automatically by a simple keyboard command.

magnetic disk *see* floppy disk, hard disk.

magnetic media Hard disks, floppy disks, and tapes coated with magnetically sensitive materials on which data can be stored; *contrasts with* nonmagnetic media (specifically, laser disks).

magnetic tape Plastic tape with a magnetized recording surface; used as a high-capacity storage medium for computer data.

mailbox In electronic mail, a storage location for messages addressed to a specific person. The messages are held in the mailbox until the person "picks them up."

mainframe A large, powerful, and expensive computer designed to process quickly enormous amounts of data.

main memory *see* primary storage.

male connector In computer cabling, a connection device that has protruding pins designed to fit into the sockets of a female connector.

management information system (MIS) A software package (often designed for a specific industry) that pulls together and summarizes data from different sources within a company; used to address managerial issues, such as: Which accounts are past due? What percentage of customer accounts are past due? How does this compare with the percentage a year ago?

manual A book sold with a hardware device or a program that explains how to install and use the purchase. Read it!

massively parallel computer A supercomputer that uses hundreds or thousands of microprocessors to perform many operations simultaneously.

mass storage *see* secondary storage.

master disk The floppy disk that a person buys from a software publisher. To protect his or her investment, the buyer should copy all the programs on the master disk onto either a working disk (for a floppy disk drive) or a working directory (for a hard disk drive), then put the original disk in a safe place.

math coprocessor A special chip, or microprocessor, added to a computer to speed up the execution of mathematical calculations; *also called* a numeric coprocessor.

media *see* magnetic media.

megabyte (M, MB, meg) A unit of measurement for computer memory; equals approximately 1 million bytes or characters (specifically, 1,048,576 bytes).

megahertz (MHz) A unit of measurement used to describe the clock speed of a computer; equals one million electrical cycles per second. For example, Intel's 80386SL microprocessor has a clock speed of 25MHz.

membrane keyboard A flat-surface keyboard with only a two-dimensional outline of each key. The surface is pressure sensitive;

a character is entered or a command is initiated when the user presses on the appropriate key outline.

memory The capacity to store data. Primary memory resides within the central processing unit (CPU) and is easily accessed; secondary, or external, memory is accessed from units such as magnetic disks or tapes.

memory management program A utility that allocates use of a computer's random access memory (RAM) and ensures that it is used efficiently.

memory map A record of what is stored in each memory address (location) in a computer's RAM and ROM.

memory-resident program An accessory or utility program that remains in a computer's memory at all times, rather than being loaded in only when needed.

menu A list of options available to the user that appears on the display screen.

menu-driven program A program that provides menus, or lists, of program options, so that a user does not have to memorize commands; *contrasts with* command-driven program.

merge To combine data from two or more files; for example, in word processing, a form letter may be merged with a list of names and addresses to create a series of "personalized" letters.

microcomputer A computer based on a microprocessor; personal computers, including desktop and laptop computers, are examples.

microprocessor A complete central processing unit (CPU) assembled on a single silicon chip.

MIDI *see* Musical Instrument Digital Interface.

million instructions per second (mips) A measurement used to describe the speed at which a central processing unit (CPU) can process instructions.

millisecond (ms) A unit of measurement of time, equal to one thousanth of a second; commonly used to indicate the access time of a hard disk drive.

minicomputer A compact computer, not much larger than a desktop microcomputer but more powerful and often designed for a particular application; frequently used as the central computer in a multiuser system.

mips *see* million instructions per second.

mirror In computer graphics, to produce a mirror image of an object or a portion of the display screen.

MIS *see* management information system.

model A mathematical or graphic representation of an object, process, concept.

modeling The use of computers to model objects and to simulate processes; for example, economic modeling enables a person to study economic growth, employment trends, housing needs, and other factors on world, national, and local levels.

modem An acronym for MOdulator/DEModulator; a device that enables a computer to send and receive data through ordinary telephone lines. It converts digital signals generated by the computer into analog signals for transmission over telephone lines, and vice versa.

module A part of a software package. It is a functionally separate unit—usually a self-contained program — but works together with other units in the package.

monitor An output device with a television-like display screen; can employ a cathode-ray tube (CRT), a liquid crystal display, or an array of light-emitting diodes; *also called* a video display terminal (VDT).

monochrome monitor A monitor that displays only one color — such as white, green, or amber — against a black background.

motherboard The main circuit board of a computer, containing the central processing unit (CPU), random-access memory, expansion slots, and other components; *also called* a logic board.

mouse An input device consisting of a palm-sized box with one or more control buttons on top; movement of the mouse across a tabletop causes a pointer on the display screen to move. A mouse typically is used to choose commands from menus, move objects on the screen, and draw pictures onscreen.

mouse pad A pad on which a mouse sits and moves about; protects a desktop and muffles noise.

MS-DOS The standard operating system of IBM and IBM-compatible 16-bit personal computers (computers that process 2 bytes — 16 bits — of information at a time); also widely used on 32-bit machines; also marketed as PC DOS.

multimedia The presentation of information using a variety of media — computer text and graphics, plus sound and video — all controlled by a computer.

multiplexer In communications, a cost-efficient linking device that bundles messages from several slow-speed input lines into one higher-speed line for transmission.

multitasking The ability of a personal computer to run two or more applications simultaneously; generally, each application is shown in its own box, or window, on the display screen.

multiuser Designed to be used by more than one person at the same time; for example, a multiuser accounting program.

multiuser system A computer system with a central computer, often a minicomputer, that can be shared (accessed) by several users (each at his or her own terminal) at the same time.

music synthesizer An electronic device with a pianolike keyboard that can duplicate — often simultaneously — the sounds of pianos, drums, guitars, and other traditional musical instruments.

Musical Instrument Digital Interface (MIDI) A protocol developed among synthesizer manufacturers that specifies how musical notes, voicing changes, and other information is exchanged between musical synthesizers and computers; requires a MIDI interface — a box or plug-in card to connect the computer and synthesizer.

N

nanosecond (ns) A unit of measurement of time, equal to one billionth of a second; commonly used to measure the speed of memory chips. For example, a 100ns RAM chip responds within 100 nanoseconds.

natural language interface A program feature that allows a person to use plain English (or another spoken language) to give commands or access information. For example, a database program may contain an internal dictionary of 1,000 words; a person uses these words to query the database.

near-letter quality (NLQ) Type produced by a printer that looks almost as good as type produced by a high-quality typewriter. Many dot matrix printers can operate in an NLQ mode.

network Two or more computers (and, usually, other hardware) that are connected together. The most common types are local area networks (LANs) and wide area networks (WANs).

network adapter card A special circuit installed in a computer to enable it to communicate with (interface with, or be part of) a local area network (LAN).

network administrator In a local area network (LAN), the person responsible for maintaining the network, installing programs on it, controlling user access to various files, etc.

network architecture *see* topology.

network drive In a local area network (LAN), a disk drive shared by all workstations; *contrasts with* local drive.

network operating system In a local area network (LAN), the software that runs the system and controls how each computer communicates on the network.

network printer In a local area network (LAN), a printer shared by all workstations; *contrasts with* local printer.

network server *see* file server.

neural network A computer modeled after the interconnected system of neurons (nerve cells) that are the basic units of the human brain. Because the network's units are interconnected, they can share data and perform their tasks simultaneously. A neural network computer also can learn from experience, teaching itself by trial and error.

node A device on a local area network (LAN); includes workstations, printers, etc.

noise Extraneous, meaningless electrical signals on a communications line; can affect data being transmitted along the line, resulting in loss of data.

non-impact printer A printer that forms an image by spraying or fusing ink onto paper. Laser, thermal, and ink-jet printers are examples.

non-volatile memory Memory that is not lost when a computer is turned off; for example, read-only memory (ROM).

notebook computer A small pc that typically weighs between 5 and 8 pounds. Even smaller computers are called subnotebooks.

number crunching Using a computer to perform a large number of calculations.

numeric coprocessor *see* math coprocessor.

numeric keypad *see* keypad.

NumLock On some keyboards with numeric keypads, a key that is used to switch the keypad keys back and forth between different functions. In default mode, the keys of the keypad function as cursor movement keys; when NumLock is pressed, the keys produce the digits 0 through 9.

nym   Among users of bulletin board systems, a slang term for pseudonym. People use nyms to ensure a degree of privacy.

O

object-oriented graphic   An image that is saved in computer memory as mathematical formulas that describe its shape, the start and end point of each line, etc. CAD programs produce object-oriented images. *Contrasts with* bit-mapped graphic.

OCR   *see* optical character reader.

OEM   *see* original equipment manufacturer.

on line   Connected to a computer and able to communicate with it. The term may be used to describe a peripheral, such as printer; a workstation in a network; or a connection via modem to a distant computer.

on-line help   In an application program, help that a user can request while using the program, perhaps by pressing a function key. For example, in a word processing program, a user may access help screens to learn how to create a table of contents for a document.

open architecture   Design specifications for a computer that are published by the manufacturer, to encourage other companies to develop peripherals and software for the machine; compare with proprietary architecture.

Open Systems Interconnection (OSI)   An international standard for the organization of local area networks (LANS), to permit equipment from different manufacturers to communicate with each other; a seven-layer model, with physical hardware connection standards addressed in the first two levels and functions such as data transport, error detection, and specific applications addressed by the upper levels.

operating system A group of programs that coordinate ongoing computer processes: loading, storing, and executing programs; input-output; networking; etc.

optical character reader (OCR) A device that scans typewritten or printed pages line by line, converting the text into binary numbers and transmitting it to a computer.

optical disk A nonmagnetic storage medium on which digital data are recorded optically by a laser beam, as minute pits and bumps; data are read by a lower-power laser beam. CD-ROM and WORM are types of optical disks; *also called* a laser disk.

optical computing A still-experimental technology in which a computer uses pulses of light rather than electrical signals to process data.

original equipment manufacturer (OEM) A company that manufactures computers, printers, modems, etc. OEMs often buy components (boards, internal disk drives, etc.) from other companies, then assemble the components.

OS/2 An acronym for Operating System/2; an operating system designed for 32-bit IBM PCs and PC-compatible computers that allows a user to run several application programs at once (a process called multitasking).

OSI *see* Open Systems Interconnection.

output Information given out by a computer. Output may be in the form of words, numbers, pictures, or sound; *contrasts with* input.

output device A peripheral that receives information from a computer, such as a monitor, printer, or speech synthesizer.

overstriking A technique used in many programs to print a character that is not part of the basic character set, such as foreign language, Greek, and math characters.

overwrite To store ("write") information at a location on a disk where information already is stored, thus destroying the original information.

P

packet A unit of data assembled into an "envelope" for transmission over a network. The envelope has an "address" that is read by a routing device at each branch in the network. The routing devices switch the packet onto the correct transmission lines until it reaches its destination.

pagination The numbering of pages. Most word processing programs allow the user to print sequential page numbers on a document, in either headers or footers.

paint/draw program A graphics program that can create both bit-mapped (paint) and object-oriented (draw) images.

paint program A graphics program that creates bit-mapped images made up of dots; every pixel on the display screen is represented ("mapped") by one or more bits. Paint programs can be used to create highly detailed, artistic graphics; *contrasts with* draw program.

palette In a graphics program, an on-screen display of symbols representing the colors and patterns that are available. When a user chooses one of the symbols (generally by using a mouse), the color or pattern becomes available for use.

palmtop computer A computer small enough to be held in the palm of one's hand, yet with many of the capabilities of a large desktop computer.

parallel port A computer interface through which the eight bits that form a byte travel in a parallel stream on eight paths. That is, all eight bits are transferred simultaneously. Most printers are connected to computers via parallel ports; *contrasts with* serial port.

parallel processing Processing of data by carrying out a series of operations simultaneously (in parallel), rather than one at a time (sequentially, or serially).

parameter A characteristic of a device or program that can be changed by the user. If the user does not specify a value or option, the system uses a default value or option. For example, the number of lines to be printed on a page is a parameter; a word processing program may set a default value of 60 lines per page but a user can easily change this to another value.

parent directory   In a root directory, the directory above the current subdirectory.

parity   A technique used to check the reliability of data transmission—for example, between a computer and its peripherals or between two computers via modem.

parity bit   An extra bit added to a character or other data field to detect errors in data transmission. If parity checking detects the loss of a bit or bits, the computer reports a parity error.

partition   A section of a hard disk; the storage area of a hard disk is divided ("partitioned") to enable faster organization of and access to data.

Pascal   A high-level, highly structured programming language that is widely used in scientific applications and for teaching programming.

password   A word that has to be entered into a computer before the user can access information, thus helping to ensure that access is restricted to authorized users. There are a variety of password options. For example, a system password allows a system to boot only after the password has been entered; a keyboard password allows a user to lock and unlock the keyboard without turning off the system.

pathname   In the root-directory structure used by MS-DOS, the series of directory names that lead to a specific file. For example, the pathname A:\WP\LETTERS\JONES4.DOC leads to a file named JONES4.DOC in the subdirectory LETTERS in the directory WP on the disk in drive A.

pc   A personal computer.

PC   An IBM pc.

peripheral A hardware device that is attached to a computer and controlled by the CPU; printers, modems, and disk drives are examples.

personal computer (PC) A general-purpose microcomputer able to run a wide variety of software.

personal information manager (PIM) Software that organizes information normally found on a person's calendars, schedules, "to do" lists, etc.

phosphor burn-in *see* ghost.

pin feed *see* tractor feed.

piracy The unauthorized — and illegal — duplication of copyrighted software.

pixel Short for "PICture ELement; a single memory location on a display screen, represented by a small dot of light. The greater the number of pixels per unit of display area, the higher the resolution. Any image on the screen is made up of a collection of pixels.

plasma display *see* gas plasma screen.

platen In impact printers, the cylinder that rolls paper through the printer and serves as a backing against which the print element strikes an image onto the paper.

plotter An output device that uses moving ink pens to print high-quality diagrams and other graphic images on paper.

plug compatible Devices that can be plugged into the same interface sockets and used interchangeably, without modification, within the computer system. For example, two printers may be plug compatible, though their internal technology, capabilities, and costs are different.

pointer A symbol (usually an arrow) on the display screen that is controlled by a mouse and is used to select menu commands or other items.

polling A method used in local area networks (LANs) to ensure that each computer can send messages or data without clashes; a central computer continuously polls the workstations, asking them if they have messages or data to transmit.

pop-up menu A list of options that appears on the screen in a location other than from a menu bar at the top of the screen; *contrasts with* pull-down menu.

port A jack or other boundary where two devices, such as a computer and a printer, are connected. The term is also used to refer to the circuit through which data are transferred between two devices. Sometimes called an interface.

portable (1) A comparatively lightweight personal computer that can be carried from one place to another. (2) A description of software that can work on various types of computer systems; for example, UNIX is a portable operating system.

power down To turn off a computer's power switch.

power surge *see* surge.

power up To turn on a computer's power switch.

presentation graphics program An application program used to create appealing charts, maps, diagrams, and other graphics used in presentations by business personnel, educators, etc. For example, such a program could take a company's sales data and create a map comparing sales growth in different parts of the country.

primary storage The part of the computer's central processing unit (CPU) that stores data and programs so that they are directly accessible for processing; synonymous with internal storage, main memory; *contrasts with* secondary storage.

printed circuit board A flat, rectangular component of a computer on which are printed the electrical connections ("circuits") among chips and other electronic parts; there are central processor boards, memory boards, communication boards, graphics boards, etc.

printer An output device that prints data from the computer, usually in text form, on paper.

printer driver A file that enables a program to send documents to a printer in a form that that specific model of printer can understand.

printout *see* hard copy.

processing The execution of program instructions by a computer's central processing unit (CPU), with the result that information is manipulated in some particular way; for example, the computer may arrange a series of names in alphabetical order, draw a bar chart, or add a column of numbers.

program (1) A list of instructions that tells a computer how to perform a specific task; *also called* software. (2) To prepare a list of instructions, or program, for a computer.

program error A mistake in a computer program, made at the time the program was written; sometimes called a bug.

programmable read-only memory (PROM) A ROM chip that can be programmed by the user. Once written, however, the memory is permanent; it can be read but not altered.

programmer A person who designs, writes, and debugs computer programs.

programming language A set of rules and commands used to write instructions for a computer. There are three basic types of programming languages: high-level languages (BASIC, COBOL, and FORTRAN are examples), assembly language, and machine language.

project management software An application program that helps to plan and track projects. It can be used to divide a project into tasks, assign people and resources to each task, schedule start and end dates and milestones for each task, etc.

PROLOG An acronym for PROgramming in LOGic; a high-level programming language; often used to create artificial intelligence programs.

PROM *see* programmable read-only memory.

prompt A message from the computer to the user indicating that it is waiting to be told what to do; usually presented as a symbol on the display screen. A blinking cursor is an example of a prompt.

proportional spacing A feature of some printers, in which wide characters such as "m" and "w" take up more space than narrow characters such as "i" and "l."

proprietary architecture Design specifications for a computer that are considered the private property of the manufacturer and may not be used by another hardware or software company unless it obtains a license; prevents companies from producing "clones" of the manufacturer's computer; compare with open architecture.

protocols Rules, or procedures, that control how data is transmitted between computers. To communicate, both computers must use the same transmission protocol(s).

public domain software Software that is not copyrighted and therefore is available to the public free of charge; *also called* freeware.

pull-down menu A list of options that appears from a menu bar at the top of the screen, "pulled down" as if it was a Venetian blind.

Q

query In a database management system, to request a particular kind of information from a database, such as all sales figures for last month or the names of customers whose accounts are overdue.

query by example (QBE) In a database management system, a feature that presents a query screen and asks the user to provide an example of the kind of information desired in each field. For example, in a field labeled "state date," a user could define overdue accounts as those that were not paid by March 1st.

QWERTY keyboard Pronounced "kwerty" and derived from the first six letters on the top alphabetic row of a typewriter; the standard typewriter keyboard layout, which also is used for computer keyboards.

R

RAM *see* random access memory.

random access The ability to go directly to a specific data location, rather than having to go through a series of locations (sequential access) before reaching the desired data. For example, a person has random access to data stored on disk and sequential access to data stored on tape.

random-access memory (RAM) The part of a computer's memory used to store data or instructions temporarily, while they are being used or changed by the user. For example, a letter being created using a word processing program is stored in RAM. The contents of RAM are lost when the computer is turned off, unless they've been saved to a disk; *compare with* read only memory.

raster graphics The display technology used in TV sets and computer monitors, in which images are composed of rows of pixels. The quality of the image is determined by the resolution (pixels per inch) and the number of shades of gray (in a monochrome image) or colors (in a color image) that a pixel can assume; *compare with* vector graphics.

raw data Data that have not yet been processed or edited; for example, a list of names that hasn't been alphabetized, expenses that haven't been entered into a spreadsheet, survey results that haven't been tabulated.

read To retrieve data or program instructions from a disk or other storage device; *contrasts with* write.

read-only memory (ROM) The part of a computer's memory used to store data or instructions that cannot easily be changed. For example, a frequently used program, such as a word processing program, may be stored in ROM. The contents of ROM are not lost when the computer is turned off; *compare with* random access memory.

read/write head The magnetic device in a hard or floppy disk drive that retrieves information from (reads) and deposits information on (writes) the disk.

real-time application A program that processes data immediately. An airline reservation system is an example: it maintains an up-to-date picture of flight data, seat availability, cancellations, etc.

reboot To boot again without turning off the power; *see* warm boot.

record In a database, a collection of related fields. For example, a customer record might include fields for company name, contact name, street address, city, state, zip code, and telephone number. A group of related records comprise a file—for example, a customer file.

record locking A networking procedure that allows two or more users to simultaneously access the same file but not the same record in that file.

reformat (1) To repeat the formatting operation on a disk, once again partitioning it into sectors and tracks. (2) In word processing, spreadsheets, and some other applications, to change the physical arrangement of text or other data on a page.

register A primary memory in the central processing unit (CPU) that acts as a temporary storage unit for data that is actually being used.

relational database A database in which information is organized in tables, similar to the way in which spreadsheets keep information; allows a user to relate data in one file to that in another file; the most common type of database structure used at present.

remote computer A computer at another location, accessible via telephone or some other communications medium.

remote computing The use of a special utility program to control another computer anywhere in the world. For example, a person working on a computer at home could access a computer in his or her office to edit a document stored on its hard disk.

repeater In local area network (LAN) and other communication lines, a device that rebroadcasts a signal; used to extend the length of a line or to increase the number of devices that can be connected to it.

report generation An application program, often part of a database management system, used to generate customized business reports.

res *shorthand for* resolution.

reset function *see* warm boot.

resident font *see* built-in font.

resolution The sharpness of an image produced by a monitor or printer. Monitor resolution usually is expressed in pixels by scan lines (640 x 480, for example); printer resolution is measured in dots per inch (132 dpi, for example). A "high-res" image is sharper than a "low-res" image.

retrieval The process of finding or getting back data. For example, to find data on a storage device or to get back data that have been accidentally erased.

return key *see* enter key.

ring topology A local area network (LAN) layout that links workstations in a closed loop; *also called* token-ring topology.

RISC An acronym for Reduced Instuction Set Computer; a chip design for central processing units (CPUs) that limits the set of instructions that the processor can execute, eliminating seldom-used instructions (which, if needed, can be part of a program). RISC chips are much faster than the more conventional CISC (Complex Instruction Set Computer) chips.

ROM *see* read only memory.

root directory The top-level directory in a directory tree, from which all other directories branch; created by MS-DOS when a disk is formatted.

rotation tool In computer graphics, a command option that allows the user to rotate an object, pivoting it around its center point to change its position.

router A device used to connect multiple local area networks (LANs); operates at the third layer of the Open Systems Interconnection (OSI) model; compare with bridge.

row In a spreadsheet, a horizontal series of cells. Rows typically are identified by sequential numbers written down the left side of the sheet; *contrasts with* column.

RS-232 A standard connector, or interface, for serial devices, such as modems.

run The execution of a computer program.

S

save To store a program or data on a disk or other storage device.

scaling In computer graphics, enlarging or reducing all or part of an image according to a specified proportion. For example, to make an image half as large it needs to be scaled at 50 percent.

scanner An input device that converts text, photographs, and other images on paper into digital (binary) form for storage within a computer sytem.

scanning (1) A technology that rapidly "reads" and digitizes images on paper. (2) In word processing, to rapidly view text by scrolling backward or forward through the document.

scissoring In computer graphics, to remove part of an image that lies outside a window or frame; *also called* clipping.

scrambler A device that encodes a message or other data being transmitted, to protect against unauthorized viewing; to be intelligible, the data must pass through an appropriately set descrambling device at the receiving end.

screen The surface of a monitor on which data are displayed.

screen dump A printout of the data displayed on the screen.

screen saver A utility program designed to protect the display screen from ghosts (phosphor burn-in). After a specified period of time during which there is no input, the program either automatically blanks the screen or displays moving images. Pressing any key or mouse button brings back the display that had been on the screen.

scroll To move text or other material either horizontally (right/left) or vertically (up/down) on the display screen.

SCSI *see* Small Computer System Interface.

search and replace *see* global search.

secondary storage An external device, such as a disk, used for the long-term storage of information; *synonymous with* auxiliary storage, external storage, and mass storage; *contrasts with* primary storage.

sector *see* track.

semiconductor A substance, such as silicon, that transmits electricity better than a resistor or insulator, but not as well as a metallic conductor; used for computer circuits.

serial port A computer interface through which the eight bits that form a byte are funneled into a one-bit-wide stream, with the eight bits in a precise order. That is, the eight bits are transferred serially. Modems and mice are among the equipment connected to a computer via serial ports; *contrasts with* parallel port.

server *see* disk server, file server.

server-based application In a local area network (LAN), an application program stored on the file server and available to more than one workstation (user) at a time.

shareware Copyrighted software that is distributed free of charge by the developer and may be legally copied and passed from one user to another. However, if after trying out the software a person decides to continue using it, he or she is expected to pay a registration fee to the developer.

sheet feeder A device that holds individual sheets of paper and automatically feeds them, one at a time, into a printer; standard equipment on some printers, optional on others.

shell A utility program designed to make it easier to use an operating system or application program. For example, an MS-DOS shell allows a person to use menus or function keys to handle common operations such as copying files, rather than having to memorize the MS-DOS commands for such operations.

shell package A software package designed to enable organizations to develop their own knowledge-based expert systems; *also called* a development tool.

shift-click A maneuver in which a Shift key on the keyboard is held down while the mouse button is clicked; used for various functions by application programs.

Shift keys Two keys on the keyboard that are used to make letters upper case and to enter certain punctuation marks. The keys have additional functions in some application programs.

SIG *see* special interest group.

silicon chip *see* chip.

simulation A computer-created model of a real or imagined situation or phenomenon; for example, airplane flight simulations and wind pattern simulations.

site license A written agreement between a software publisher and an organization that allows the organization to make copies of a program for use within the organization. The license usually indicates the number of copies that may be made.

slot *see* expansion slot.

Small Computer Systems Interface (SCSI) An interface standard for high-speed peripherals such as hard disk drives and laser printers; the acronym is pronounced "scuzzy."

SmallTalk A high-level, graphics-oriented programming language; uses include the creation of artificial intelligence programs.

smart terminal A terminal in a multiuser system that has its own central processing unit (CPU) and disk drive(s). In addition to retrieving data and sending data to a host computer it can edit, store data, etc.; *contrasts with* dumb terminal.

soft copy The copy of the computer's output — a document, graph, or other data — that appears on the display screen; "soft" in the sense that it is easily changed, replaced, or erased; *contrasts with* hard copy.

software A computer program; the instructions that tell a computer what to do; *contrasts with* hardware.

software package A ready-to-use program or collection of programs, together with documentation and any other necessary support.

sort To rearrange the order of data; for example, in a database of baseball players, sorting alphabetically by name or numerically by batting averages.

source code A computer program as it is written in a high-level programming language (before it has been compiled or interpreted into machine code).

source file The file on a disk from which data or program instructions are copied into the computer for processing; *contrasts with* destination file.

special interest group (SIG) A group of people who share an interest in a particular type of hardware or software or a particular aspect of computing, such as accounting or graphics; often part of a larger organization, such as a user group or bulletin board system.

special-purpose computer A computer designed for one particular purpose, such as studying weather phenomena; *contrasts with* general-purpose computer.

speech recognition The ability of a computer system to recognize words spoken by humans.

speech synthesis The ability of a computer system to produce an audio output that resembles human speech.

spell checker A program that checks the spelling of words in a document. Each word in the document is compared to words in a previously recorded file; any document words not found in the file are queried.

spike *see* surge.

spreadsheet An application program that simulates an accountant's worksheet; performs mathematical operations on numbers arranged in columns and rows; used mainly for accounting and other record keeping.

SRAM *see* static random access memory.

start bit In telecommunications, a special bit sent to let a modem know that it is about to receive data bits.

star topology A local area network (LAN) in which workstations are linked in a starlike layout, with the workstations radiating out from a central computer that serves as a controller.

static random access memory (SRAM) A memory chip that stores information on a short-term basis and does not have to be constantly recharged.

status line In an application program, a line displayed on the screen that provides important information about the file currently being processed. For example, the status line in a word processing program may indicate the directory path and name of the file, whether word wrap is on or off, and the percentage of computer memory still available for editing.

stop bit In telecommunications, a special bit sent immediately after the data bits for a character have been transmitted.

storage capacity The maximum amount of information that can be held in a computer or a storage device at any one time; for example, an 80MB computer has a main memory capacity of 80MB of data.

storage device A magnetic or optical device used for the long-term storage of information; examples include floppy disks, CD-ROM, and tape.

string A series of alphanumeric characters that are treated as a unit; for example, a number or a person's name.

Structured Query Language (SQL) A query language created for accessing and manipulating data in databases. Its standardized commands are designed to allow its use with databases on micro-computers, minicomputers, and mainframes. The acronym is pronounced "see-quel."

style checker *see* grammar checker.

stylus *see* electronic stylus.

subdirectory A directory located within another directory. For example, a directory listing all the files on a disk might have sub-directories labeled "Letters," "Reports," and "Speeches."

submenu A menu located within another menu. For example, a help menu in a word processing program may have submenus labeled "Spell Checker" and "Formatting Page Layout."

subroutine A self-contained module in a program that performs a specific task.

supercomputers The fastest, most powerful, and most expensive computers.

super-VGA (SVGA) An enhanced version of the VGA color graphics display standard for IBM PC and PC-compatible computers; provides a resolution of up to 1064 pixels horizontally by 768 pixels vertically.

surge A brief increase in electric power, or voltage, that can damage computers and other electronic equipment; often caused by lightning or by the return of power after a power outage; *also called* a spike.

surge protector An electrical device that prevents high-voltage surges from reaching a computer and damaging its components; *also called* a surge suppressor.

synchronous communication The high-speed transmission of data in the form of blocks called packets; the packets are sent at regular intervals timed to synchronize with the modem clock of the host computer; *compare with* asynchronous communication.

syntax (1) The order in which a user must type a command—for example, to the operating system—plus any parameters that follow the command. (2) In programming, the rules that govern how program statements must be spelled, punctuated, and structured so that a computer can recognize and process the instructions.

synthesizer A device that produces certain sounds, such as a music synthesizer or a speech synthesizer.

sysop An acronym for SYStem OPerator; pronounced "siss-op;" the person who maintains a bulletin board.

system disk Any disk that contains the part of the operating system needed to start a computer; *also called* a boot disk or start-up disk.

systems analyst A person who identifies the specific functions, or tasks, to be performed by a computer system and helps to design and implement the system.

system software All the software used to control the operation of a computer system; includes the operating system and supporting utility programs.

T

Tab key A key on the keyboard used to advance the cursor to a predetermined location on the line, called a tab stop. The Tab key is useful for indenting the beginning of paragraphs, creating columns of data, etc. (Word processing and other application programs allow the user to customize the locations of tab stops.)

tape *see* magnetic tape.

tape backup unit A storage device used to copy (back up) onto magnetic tape the files contained on a hard disk; may be a separate unit or built into the computer. Backing up on tape is a much faster and less error-prone procedure than backing up on floppy disks.

tape cartridge In a tape backup unit, a reel of high-quality magnetic tape enclosed in a plastic case.

technical support Assistance provided by a hardware or software manufacturer to registered users of a product; for example, technical support provided by a computer manufacturer may include advice on how to install a second disk drive.

telecommunications The transfer of information over telephone lines; includes both voice and computer data.

telecommuting Working at home and communicating with the office via computer and modem.

template (1) In some application programs, a generic pattern that can be used repeatedly and, if desired, customized; for example, letterhead templates in word processing programs and mortgage amortization schedules in spreadsheets. (2) A guide that fits over a keyboard and lays out key commands for a particular software package.

terabyte (TB) A unit of measurement for computer memory; equals approximately one trillion bytes or characters (specifically, 1,099,511,627,766 bytes).

terminal An input/output device connected to a central computer in a multiuser system; *see also* dumb terminal, smart terminal.

terminate and stay resident (TSR) program An accessory or utility program that, once loaded, remains in the computer's random access memory (RAM) and can be rapidly activated by the user; desk managers are examples.

text Words, letters, and numbers; *contrasts with* graphics.

text file *see* ASCII file.

thermal printer A non-impact printer that uses heated styluses to burn characters and graphic images onto special heat-sensitive paper.

thesaurus *see* electronic thesaurus.

third-party vendor A company that markets hardware or software designed to work with a certain brand of computer; for example, a company (other than IBM) that sells monitors that work with IBM computers.

three-dimensional spreadsheet A spreadsheet that has various pages as well as rows and columns; for example, a spreadsheet for a store's sales figures could be organized by product (rows: first dimension), time (columns: second dimension), and departments (pages: third dimension).

timed backup In many application programs, a feature that automatically saves a file at specified intervals, such as every 5 minutes or every time the user has typed 2,000 characters.

time-sharing The simultaneous use of a large central computer by two or more people who are working independently, at separate terminals; the central computer and the users may be at separate locations.

toggle To switch back and forth between two modes by pressing the same key or combination of keys. For example, in word processing, a user toggles *italic type* on and off—the first time the user presses the toggle key(s), italicizing begins; the next time the toggle key(s) are pressed, italicizing ends.

token passing A scheme used in a ring network to allow workstations to gain access to the network. A token—which consists of a pattern of bits—is either free or busy. A workstation that wants to send a message can capture a free token and change it to indicate a message is on its way through the system. After the message has been received and acknowledged, the token's value is reset to free.

token-ring topology   *see* ring topology.

topology   The architecture of a local area network (LAN); how computers and other hardware are connected and how information flows in the LAN; examples include bus, ring, and star topologies, as well as hybrid arrangements.

touch-sensitive display   A display technology that allows a user, by touching the pressure-sensitive screen at the appropriate place, to instruct the computer to perform a certain operation.

track   One of many concentric circles on a floppy disk or hard disk, encoded by the operating system when the disk is formatted. Each track is divided into sectors, which are the basic units of storage space for data.

trackball   An input device designed as an alternative to a mouse. Unlike a mouse, it does not move; instead, a user moves a pointer or cursor on the display screen by spinning the small ball with his or her fingers.

tractor feed   A printer mechanism using sprockets that fit into prepunched holes on the right and left edges of the paper; enables the printer to print on continuous-form (fan-fold) paper; *synonymous with* pin feed; *contrasts with* friction feed.

traffic   In communications, the volume of data sent over a line.

transistor   A device, made of silicon or another semiconducting material, that can control the flow of electrons, enabling it to act as a switching device to record information in the form of an "on" or an "off" signal.

translate   To convert a program written in assembly language or a high-level language into machine language that the computer can understand. Assemblers, compilers, and interpreters are translation programs.

Trojan horse A program designed to perform a secret function in addition to its advertised purpose. For example, it may display cute graphics on the display screen while secretly erasing the files on the hard disk. Trojan horses are serious computer security threats.

TSR *see* terminate and stay resident program.

turnkey system A complete computer system, including software, packaged by a value-added reseller (VAR) for a specific application, such as a dentist's office or a restaurant. The VAR generally installs the system, turning it over to the customer ready to be used.

tutorial (1) Instructions designed to help a person learn how to use a program by guiding him or her step-by-step through an application using imaginary data; for example, writing a letter with a word processing program or setting up and retrieving information from a database with a database program. (2) A major type of educational software, designed to teach students new information; for example, a tutorial on genetics.

twisted-pair cable An inexpensive type of transmission medium, commonly used in telephone systems. The cable contains two insulated wires wrapped ("twisted") around each other.

typeface The distinctive design of a set of type; for example, typefaces built into a dot-matrix printer may include draft, Roman, and sans serif.

type size The size of a font, measured in points. For example, in the font 10-point Helvetica, Helvetica is the typeface and 10 point is the type size.

U

undo A command available in some application programs that cancels the results of a previous command. For example, in a word processing program, an undo command might restore a document to its appearance just prior to a formatting command.

uninterruptible power supply (UPS) A battery-powered device that provides a constant supply of current to a computer in the event of a power failure, giving the user perhaps 5 or 10 minutes in which to complete a task and save work to a disk.

UNIX A multiuser, multitasking operating system designed to run on a wide variety of computers, from microcomputers to mainframes.

upgrade (1) To expand or improve a computer system. (2) To replace a program with a newer or more powerful version.

upload To send a program or other data via a modem to another computer; for example, a person may upload a document to a bulletin board; *contrasts with* download.

UPS *see* uninterruptible power supply.

upward compatible Describes software that is able to work, without modifications, on newer computer systems or operating systems than those for which it was originally created; for example, a program written for the original Macintosh that can also be run on later Macintosh models.

user The person who uses a computer for word processing, communications, and other applications; *synonymous with* end user; *contrasts with* programmer, retailer, etc.

user ID A name or number used for identification when entering (logging on to) a bulletin board system or information service.

user friendly Hardware and software that is easy to use by people who lack extensive computer experience or training.

user group A club of computer users; usually consists of people who use the same kind of hardware or software—such as a group of Mac owners or Lotus 1-2-3 users. Members of a user group share information, hear presentations by experts, exchange public domain software, etc.

user interface The features of a computer or a program that determine how it interacts with a user. For example, menus and commands are part of the user interface.

utility A program designed to perform certain housekeeping or maintenance tasks, such as formatting disks, examining the contents of a file directory, and recovering accidentally deleted files. Utilities improve the efficiency of a computer system.

V

vaccine A utility program designed to detect and destroy computer viruses; *also called* an antivirus program.

value-added reseller (VAR) A vendor who combines hardware and software, usually from various manufacturers, for resale as a complete turnkey system. The package price generally includes installation, training, and customer support.

vaporware A slang term for software promised by a company but never actually released.

VAR *see* value-added reseller.

VDT *see* monitor.

VDT radiation Low-level electromagnetic radiation emitted by computer monitors (video display terminals, or VDTs). Research suggests that there may be a link between long-term exposure to VDT radiation and health problems such as miscarriages.

vector graphics A display technology in which images are specified as a series of lines; an image is stored in computer memory as a list of coordinates for the start and end points of each line (called a display list). Vector graphics have professional uses, in such fields as architecture and engineering; *compare with* raster graphics.

vector-to-raster conversion A utility that transforms object-oriented (vector) images into bit-mapped (raster) images.

vendor A person or business that sells hardware, software, or computer-related services.

version A specific release of a program. It usually is given a version number to differentiate it from earlier versions of the same program; for example, PC-Write 4.0 is a newer version than PC-Write 3.0.

vertical application Software designed for a specific market, such as architects, dairy farmers, or retailers.

very large-scale integration (VLSI) chip A silicon chip that contains 100,000 or more transistors.

VGA An acronym for Video Graphics Array. A color graphics display standard for IBM PC and PC-compatible computers that provides a resolution of 640 pixels horizontally by 480 pixels vertically and displays as many as 256 colors simultaneously; replaced earlier CGA and EGA standards; *see also* super-VGA.

videoconferencing A meeting conducted via telephone and television; people (conferees) in different locations can see and hear one another.

video display terminal (VDT) *see* monitor.

video monitor *see* monitor.

virtual reality A developing area of computer technology; uses computers to create the illusion that the user is actually inside a three-dimensional simulation of an environment (for example, a coral reef, Mesozoic swamp, or human blood system). The user wears equipment that senses his or her movements, which act as commands to the program; also known as artificial reality.

virus A computer program or program segment that can attach itself to another program, reproduce itself, and spread from one program to another. Viruses, which are illegal, are often destructive, changing data and in other ways sabotaging computer systems.

VLSI *see* very large-scale integration chip.

voice mail A communication system that changes spoken telephone messages into digital form (1s and 0s), then converts the digital signals back to sound when the receiver logs on to the system to "pick up" his or her mail.

voice recognition The ability of a computer, through a special input device, to translate spoken words into digital signals.

voice synthesis The production by a computer of speech that imitates the human voice.

volatile memory Memory that is cleared, or lost, when a computer is turned off; for example, random-access memory (RAM).

volume label In some operating systems, such as MS-DOS, a name that identifies a disk ("volume"); given to the disk at the time it is formatted and displayed on the screen with a directory command; comparable to a hand-written label put on the outside of the disk.

W

WAN *see* wide area network.

warm boot To restart, or reset, a computer without turning off the computer, by pressing a special key or series of keys. This clears the memory and reloads the operating system; *contrasts with* cold boot.

what-if analysis In spreadsheet programs, the ability to explore alternatives simply by changing certain key variables and letting the program recalculate the results; for example, observing what happens to a company's profits when monthly inflation rates change.

what-you-see-is-what-you-get (WYSIWYG) pronounced "wizzy wig"; the ability of some word processing programs and other software to display documents on the screen in exactly the same format as they will be printed.

wide area network (WAN) A computer network that uses telephone lines and satellites to connect computers over distances greater than those possible with local area networks (LANs).

wildcard A character used to represent another character or group of characters that may occupy the same position. There are two wildcards in MS-DOS: the asterisk (*) and the question mark (?), which are useful when specifying directory paths and files. For example, a DIR REPORT*.TXT command asks the computer to list all directory entries with filenames that begin with "report" and have the extension TXT.

Winchester   A type of hard disk drive that has a sealed housing to prevent contamination of the disk and read/write head.

window   A rectangular area on a divided display screen, through which a person can view and work on a document, database, or other application. Many programs and some operating systems divide the screen into windows, thereby allowing users to simultaneously look at different parts of a program or file—or at parts of several programs or files. Windows can be opened, moved, overlapped, enlarged, and closed.

word processing   An application program designed for manipulating written text; used for writing, editing, and rewriting.

word wrap   The automatic movement of a word too long to fit on a line to the next line; a feature of word processing programs and other programs that generate text.

workstation   (1) A high-performance microcomputer specialized for use in a particular field, such as engineering or graphics. (2) A microcomputer in a local area network (LAN).

WORM   *see* write-once-read-many.

write   To store data on a disk or other storage device; *contrasts with* read.

write-once-read-many (WORM)   A laser-based, optical storage system that allows a user to write data onto a disk once, access the data repeatedly, but not alter or erase the data.

write protect   An option that allows a user to read from a floppy disk but prevents writing to the disk or erasing data stored on the disk. A 5.25-inch disk has a notch cut in its side; covering the notch with a sticker provides write protection. A 3.5-inch disk has a small plastic tab that slides over a hole for write protection.

WYSIWYG   *see* what-you-see-is-what-you-get.

X-Y-Z

X.25 The standard developed by the Comité Consultatif International Téléphonique et Télégraphique (CCITT) for connecting computers to a public network that uses packet switching.

X.400 The standard developed by the Comité Consultatif International Téléphonique et Télégraphique (CCITT) for electronic mail services; it defines how messages should be transferred within a network or between networks.

XENIX A version of the UNIX operating system designed to run on microcomputers.

XModem In asynchronous communications, a transmission protocol used for sending files between computers; sends a file in packets, with each packet containing 128K of data; can transfer one file at a time.

YModem In asynchronous communications, a transmission protocol used for sending files between computers; sends a file in packets, with each packet containing 1,024K of data; can transfer multiple files at one time.

zap To erase or delete.

ZModem In asynchronous communications, a transmission protocol used for sending files between computers; can transfer multiple files at one time; considerably faster and more accurate than Kermit, XModem, and YModem (other major protocols used for file transfers).

zoom (1) To adjust the size of a window on the display screen, making it either larger or smaller. (2) In a graphics program, to adjust the size of a drawing, bringing it closer to or farther away from the viewer to reveal more or less detail.